WHY AM JOY:FULLY LUTHERAN?

Instruction, Meditation, and Prayers on Luther's Small Catechism

BY MATTHEW C. HARRISON

CONCORDIA PUBLISHING HOUSE · SAINT LOUIS

Dedicated to the great pastors, teachers, church workers,
and people of The Lutheran Church—Missouri Synod

*. . . always in every prayer of mine for you all
making my prayer with joy.*
Philippians 1:4

CONTENTS

FOREWORD

Why am I Joy:fully Lutheran? I've thought and written about the topic of Christian joy previously and am humbled and gratified that *A Little Book on Joy: The Secret of Living a Good News Life in a Bad News World* (CPH 2011) has been so well received. In the devotional section of that book, I set forth a plan ("The Great Ninety Days of Joy after Joy") for praying biblical texts on joy from Ash Wednesday through the ascension of Jesus. There (pp. 181–84), I shared Luther's simple but profoundly helpful method for praying the catechism or any biblical or Christian texts, and we are reprinting those pages in this book (see appendix). For years, I'd been familiar with Luther's admonition to pray the catechism but had no idea what he actually meant. Then I read his "Simple Way to Pray" (AE 43:189–209.). Luther wrote the little pamphlet for his barber, Peter. Since then, I had the pleasure of rendering a fresh translation of this document for Concordia Publishing House. I've incorporated Luther's method in the devotional prayers in the book now in your hands, dear reader. In short, Luther would consider a text, such as a commandment or a petition of the Lord's Prayer, and then focus his prayer in four ways: (1) How does this text **instruct** me with respect to God's Word? (2) What **thanks** do I give to God for the topic of this text? (3) What sins do I have to **confess** in light of this text? (4) A concluding prayer for grace and faith to be a Christian with respect to the topic of the text. Luther's method coincides remarkably with apostolic admonition: "Rejoice always, pray without ceasing, give thanks in all circumstances; for this is the will of God in Christ Jesus for you" (1 Thessalonians 5:16–18).

Do concentrate on Luther's method. His insight into the relationship of praying set words and also allowing the Holy Spirit to prompt godly and free prayer is pure and faithful genius.

I decided to take up the joy topic again, but in a couple of specific ways in this little book. In *A Little Book on Joy*, I was intent on sharing something of the plethora of biblical texts on joy, confident that the living and active Word of God accomplishes what it says. Despite the myriad challenges of life, the Word of God gives an even more extensive and fulsome cause for joy and, by grace (the Greek word for "joy" has the same root as that of "grace"), actually renders the Christian joyous.

This book takes a different path. In answering the question, "Why am I Joy:fully Lutheran?" I decided to write a devotional treatment of the Six Chief Parts of the Catechism with Luther's commentary on the Small Catechism, now in English and published by CPH. The text of this book waxes with instruction, reflection, and prayer interspersed. The Small Catechism's treatment of the basics of the faith—the Ten Commandments, the Creed, the Lord's Prayer, Baptism, Confession and Absolution, and the Lord's Supper—is full of consolation and a tremendous cause for joy. The reader will note that the Small Catechism is replete with internal cross-references between the articles of faith. So, there is salutary but hardly tedious repetition.

In working through the catechism this way, I discovered something that should have been patently obvious to me. The catechism is through and through a remedy for the troubled conscience, the greatest enemy of Christian joy. Sin ravages relationships with God and fellow human beings. That indeed was Luther's greatest struggle, and sure comfort for the troubled and doubting conscience was and is the point of the whole Lutheran Reformation. I come away from this endeavor ever more convinced of the simple and sure clarity of the Bible, and especially its clarity on its basic teachings as the remedy for hurting and joyless souls. It is my sincere prayer that you come away from this text more confident than ever in the Gospel of Christ's free forgiveness, doled out *for you*, in nonabstract, concrete ways with absolute, divinely wrought certainty. For that, in short, is precisely what it means to be fully Lutheran, and joyfully so: Joy:fully Lutheran.

I've limited quotations mostly to the Bible and to Luther's Large Catechism (LC), with a few passages here and there from the Lutheran Confessions, which provide pertinent insight. I have not tried to provide absolute uniformity in the length of each treatment, but have followed where the catechism texts lead. Psalm 16:11 is my prayer for you.

You make known to me the path of life; in Your presence there is fullness of joy; at Your right hand are pleasures forevermore. (PSALM 16:11)

Pastor Matthew C. Harrison

ABBREVIATIONS

AC	Augsburg Confession
AE	American Edition of Luther's Works
ANF	The Ante-Nicene Fathers
Ap	Apology of the Augsburg Confession
Ep	Epitome of the Formula of Concord
FC	Formula of Concord
LC	Large Catechism of Martin Luther
LSB	*Lutheran Service Book*
NPNF	Nicene and Post-Nicene Fathers
SA	Smalcald Articles
SC	Small Catechism of Martin Luther
SD	Solid Declaration of the Formula of Concord
Tr	Treatise on the Power and Primacy of the Pope
WA	Weimar Edition of Luther's Works

THE TEN COMMANDMENTS

As the head of the family should teach them
in a simple way to his household

CHAPTER 1

The First Commandment
You shall have no other gods.

> *What does this mean?* We should fear, love, and trust in God above all things.

My heart exults in the LORD. **(1 SAMUEL 2:1)**

The First Commandment is the greatest. My encounter with it will determine whether I shall try to satisfy myself with pseudojoys or be crushed, raised, and then rendered joyful by the timeless and profound joy of the one eternal God, Father, Son, and Holy Spirit.

Who or what shall be my god? To whom or what shall I look for blessing, confidence, security? What do I desire? What do I fear? What do I love? What do I trust? All the Commandments are bound together in this First. That's why Luther begins the explanation of each with, "We should fear, love, and trust in God so that . . ." Each of the Commandments follows the First in laying bare and mercilessly condemning our common idols and gods.

> What does it mean to have a god? Or, what is God? Answer: A god means that from which we are to expect all good and in which we are to take refuge in all distress. So, to have a God is nothing other than trusting and believing Him with the heart. I have often said that the confidence and faith of the heart alone make both God and an idol. If your faith and trust is right, then your god is also true. On the other hand, if your trust is false and wrong, then you do not have the true God. For these two belong together, faith and God [Hebrews 11:6]. Now I say that whatever you set your heart on and put your trust in is truly your god. (LC I 2–3)

False gods offer false joys. Idols are infinite. Like a thousand local gods, or the pantheon of the ancient Greeks or modern Hindus, the plethora of idolatrous possibilities beckons the unwary sinner and would-be saint. "He who has money and possessions feels secure and is joyful and undismayed as though he were sitting in the midst of paradise. . . . This care and desire for money sticks and clings to our nature, right up to the grave" (LC I 7, 9). Great point, Luther. "For we brought nothing into the world, and we cannot take anything out of the world" (1 Timothy 6:7; see Job 1:21; Ecclesiastes 5:15). Infinite are the stories of joyless millionaires. But we're all in the same boat. I've seen obscene greed most virulent in unscrupulous beggars. I should be a fool and a liar to deny my own wretchedness. Money makes a very poor god. It has to be locked up and protected and worried about!

Shall your idol be "skill, prudence, power, favor, friendship, and honor" (LC I 10)? Shall your idols follow the pattern of the Ten Commandments—name and recognition? adulation? power? strength? fear of failing health? sex? lust for what's not yours? reputation at the expense of others? being the one who knows the scuttle? desire for things? They all promise joy. Shall your idols be your presumed holiness? your sanctity? your religiosity? your sanctimonious self-righteousness? The "pleasure" is short-lived. The fix is fleeting. The addictions remain unsatisfied. The gods are false. They are blind, deaf, and dumb. They hear no prayers. Their consolation is illusionary. They die with us.

The First Commandment requires faith in the one true God, Father, Son, and Holy Spirit. In the blazing brilliance of the light it shines on my wretched life, I see in myself—that is, in my sinful flesh—fear, love, and trust in just about anyone or anything *but* the one true God. I see in my life and actions the profound truth expressed by St. Augustine: "Thou hast formed us for Thyself, and our hearts are restless till they find rest in Thee" (*Confessions* 1.1.4; *NPNF* 1/1:45). I would say, "Our hearts are joyless until they find joy in You." Sin is always the propping

13

up of false gods for the sake of pseudojoys and fleeting pleasures. We are so prone to it, so blind to our faults, so ready to deny our perpetual infractions that we have no real understanding of the seriousness of our plight. The Lord Himself said, "The intention of man's heart is evil from his youth" (Genesis 8:21). In fact, our sinfulness is so profound a malady that it cannot be comprehended. It must be revealed to us by Holy Scripture and believed.[1] Witness how profoundly difficult it is even to get two Christians who have heard the Word of God for a lifetime and who have sinned against each other to ask for forgiveness and forgive!

Hebrews 1:9 says of Jesus, "You have loved righteousness and hated wickedness; therefore God, Your God, has anointed You with the oil of joy beyond Your companions." He "loved righteousness" by being perfect in thought, word, and deed. "For we do not have a high priest who is unable to sympathize with our weaknesses, but one who in every respect has been tempted as we are, yet without sin" (Hebrews 4:15). In His earthly walk, Jesus feared, loved, and trusted God the Father above all things. "And being found in human form, He humbled Himself by becoming obedient to the point of death, even death on a cross" (Philippians 2:8).

His perfect keeping of the Law for us is starkly demonstrated in Gethsemane: "Father, if You are willing, remove this cup from Me. Nevertheless, not My will, but Yours, be done" (Luke 22:42). He both kept the First Commandment and suffered the punishment we deserve for not keeping it! "But He was pierced for our transgressions; He was crushed for our iniquities; upon Him was the chastisement that brought us peace, and with His wounds we are healed" (Isaiah 53:5).

---

1   "This hereditary sin is such a deep corruption of nature that no reason can understand it. Rather, it must be believed from the revelation of Scripture. (See Psalm 51:5; Romans 6:12–13; Exodus 33:3; Genesis 3:7–19.)" (SA III 1 3).

Why am I Joy:fully Lutheran?

Because Jesus kept the First Commandment for me. He suffered my just punishment for all my sins against the First Commandment. Freed from the results of my own sin, freed from eternal death and the devil, freed from idolatry, I rejoice! "Restore to me the joy of Your salvation, and uphold me with a willing spirit" (Psalm 51:12). And finally, freed from idolatrous abuse of all that is not God, I can use and enjoy God's wonderful creation not as fake gods, the objects of my fear, love, and trust, but precisely as joyous gifts.

Dear Lord, in Your blessed Scriptures, You **instruct** us that You, Father, Son, and Spirit, are alone God. You mandate that we should have no other gods and that we fear, love, and trust You only.

I **thank** You that in the perfect life and sacrificial death of Jesus, You have redeemed me from all my sins, all of which are idolatry—the worship of false gods.

I **confess** that I continue daily to sin much in thought, word, and deed and indeed deserve nothing but punishment.

Forgive me. Renew my heart. Slay the old Adam within me. Destroy my idols. Cause me to cling to Jesus only, rejoice in Him alone, and find faithful joy in the right use of all Your creation. Amen.

CHAPTER 2

The Second Commandment
You shall not misuse the name of the Lord your God.

> *What does this mean?* We should fear and love God so that we do not curse, swear, use satanic arts, lie, or deceive by His name, but call upon it in every trouble, pray, praise, and give thanks.

> But let all who take refuge in You rejoice; let them ever sing for joy, and spread Your protection over them, that those who love Your name may exult in You. **(PSALM 5:11)**

The First Commandment instructs the heart and faith. The Second instructs the mouth and lips (LC I 50). "What comes out of the mouth proceeds from the heart" (Matthew 15:18).

The sacred name of God, "Yahweh," first appears in Genesis 2, as the Word of God details the wondrous creation of man and woman. "Then the Lord [Yahweh] God formed the man of dust from the ground and breathed into his nostrils the breath of life, and the man became a living creature" (Genesis 2:7). Man is created to know who the Lord God is and to walk with Him. Man is created with a joyous heart and lips to express that jubilation. The fall into sin—the great killjoy—is followed by the promise of the Gospel and the first naming of the Savior to come.

> I will put enmity between you and the woman, and between your offspring [seed] and her offspring [Seed]; He shall bruise your head, and you shall bruise His heel. (Genesis 3:15)

Sin ravages and disorients. Just twelve chapters into Genesis, by the time of Abraham (ca. 2000 BC), the name of God—Yahweh—had been all but forgotten. Yahweh revealed Himself to

Abraham and snatched him out of idolatry (see Genesis 12:1; Joshua 24:2). Yahweh promised Abraham, "In your offspring shall all the nations of the earth be blessed" (Genesis 22:18). Yahweh revealed Himself half a millennium later to Moses in the burning bush. "And the Angel of the LORD [Yahweh] appeared to him in a flame of fire out of the midst of a bush" (Exodus 3:2). Moses received his marching orders to lead the people of God out of bondage in Egypt. But Moses asked, Who shall I say sent me to do this? "God said to Moses, I AM WHO I AM" (Exodus 3:14). The name of Yahweh is the strong cord that laces together the great creating and savings acts of God, which themselves are intertwined with the promises, types, and prophetic precursors to Christ throughout the Old Testament.

The long story reaches its climax with the New Testament confession "Jesus is LORD." That is to say, "Jesus is Yahweh." St. Paul asserts it by referencing Joel 2:32, "Everyone who calls on the name of the LORD will be saved," connecting that verse to Jesus (Romans 10:13)! "If you confess with your mouth that Jesus is Lord and believe in your heart that God raised Him from the dead, you will be saved. For with the heart one believes and is justified, and with the mouth one confesses and is saved" (Romans 10:9–10). "As we have heard in the First Commandment— the heart by faith gives God the honor due Him first. Afterward, the lips give Him honor by confession" (LC I 70). God has revealed Himself fully and finally in Jesus. Jesus Himself revealed the "name" for us. "Go therefore and make disciples of all nations, baptizing them in the *name* of the Father and of the Son and of the Holy Spirit" (Matthew 28:19; emphasis added).

How often my lips fail. How often, in a fit of sinful delusion, words, even the divine name, have crossed my lips in anger. When I remain silent or mask my anger with words less revealing of my sinful disposition, my mind betrays me. I fear ridicule or being identified with Christ and easily curse and swear with Peter, "I do not know the man!" (Matthew 26:72, 74). I am a Christian. I bear Christ's name, but drag that name through every sinful thought, word, and deed, often in full view of others. I'm free, but I fail to confess, as though I were a bondman awaiting a whipping instead of joyful blessings. What overwhelming deceit would deny that I've lied. How cold my heart is at prayer. How sparse, empty, and fleeting my praise. How thankless I am, though showered with infinite blessings, temporal and eternal. Joyless.

Christ, be my sin (see 2 Corinthians 5:21)! Christ, be my righteousness! Christ, be my lips! Christ, intercede for me! Christ, speak my prayer! "Forgive them, Lord, they know not . . ." (see Luke 23:34). O Christ, sing praise for my stammering lips! "I confess You, Father . . ." (see Matthew 11:4). O Father in heaven, look to Christ and hear His thanksgiving. "After He gave thanks He broke it and gave it . . ." (see Luke 22:19).

Over against my wretchedness, I plead the *name*. Only the *name*.

"One little word can fell him," Luther sang against the devil (*LSB* 656:3). That "little word" is the name of God in the flesh, Jesus. "His name is a refuge like a mighty fortress . . . to which the righteous flee and are protected" (WA 38:365).

WHY AM I JOY:FULLY LUTHERAN?

I know God by His name. I know Jesus.

O Jesus, **instruct** me in Your Word and truth. "Your word is truth" (Psalm 119:160; John 17:17).

O Lord, let me "offer sacrifices of **thanksgiving**, and tell of [Your] deeds in songs of joy!" (Psalm 107:22).

O Jesus, give my heart and mouth the humility to **confess** my sins and the strength to confess Your name!

O Jesus, "open my lips" (Psalm 51:15) to pray unceasingly for Your blessings.

CHAPTER 3

The Third Commandment
Remember the Sabbath day by keeping it holy.

> *What does this mean?* We should fear and love God so that we do not despise preaching and His Word, but hold it sacred and gladly hear and learn it.

Then I will go to the altar of God, to God my exceeding joy, and I will praise You with the lyre, O God, my God. **(PSALM 43:4)**

Over the centuries, not a few Christians, including some Lutherans, have missed the joyful and central truth of the Third Commandment. It must be understood in the full light of the Gospel, in the light of Christ, "lord of the Sabbath" (Matthew 12:8). In the Old Testament, work was forbidden. Rest was given for man and beast. By the time of Jesus, tradition had been piled high; the commandment itself—including the joyous nature of the Sabbath (Isaiah 58:13)—had been obscured. The simplest acts of life were forbidden in a legalistic fit of apparent religious scrupulosity. Even Jesus was attacked by the super religious for allegedly playing fast and loose with the Sabbath! "Look, Your disciples are doing what is not lawful to do on the Sabbath" (Matthew 12:2).

Rest *is* beneficial. The Bible's testimony that God created the earth in six days and rested on the seventh (Genesis 1; 2:1–3) has wonderfully shaped the world's marking of time in the work week. But Martin Luther, the professor of Old Testament, keenly recognized that Christ and the New Testament do not require a Sabbath rest on a specific day as did the old covenant. "The word *holiday* is used for the Hebrew word *sabbath*, which properly means 'to rest,' that is, to cease from labor. Therefore, we usually say, 'to stop working.' Or 'Sanctify the Sabbath.' . . . This commandment, therefore, in its literal sense, does not apply to us Christians" (LC I 79, 82).

The "Lord's day" (Revelation 1:10), or "the first day of the week" (Acts 20:7), when Christ was raised from the dead, is Sunday, not the Old Testament Sabbath Day, Saturday. From earliest times in the church, the tradition has been to gather on Sunday to hear the Word preached and receive Christ's gifts. As the blessed apostle Paul himself testifies, Christ brought a completely new and joyful reality:

> You, who were dead in your trespasses and the uncircumcision of your flesh, God made alive together with Him, having forgiven us all our trespasses, by canceling the record of debt that stood against us with its legal demands. This He set aside, nailing it to the cross. . . . Therefore let no one pass judgment on you in questions of food and drink, or with regard to a festival or a new moon or a Sabbath. These are a shadow of the things to come, but the substance belongs to Christ. (Colossians 2:13–14, 16–17)

Luther marvelously summarized the New Testament significance of the Third Commandment in his great hymn "These Are the Holy Ten Commands."

The day off work provides much-needed rest for man and beast. But the most significant thing on such days is that "we have the freedom and time to attend divine service. We come together to hear and use God's Word, and then to praise God, to sing and to pray" (LC I 84).

. . . so that we do not despise preaching and His Word,

Why is it so important that "we do not despise preaching and His Word"? It is because "God's Word is the true 'holy thing' [relic] above all holy things. . . . Wherever God's Word is taught, preached, heard, read, or meditated upon, then the person, day, and work are sanctified" (LC I 91–92). God's Word brings the gifts of which it speaks. "Faith comes by hearing, and hearing through the word of Christ" (Romans 10:17).

. . . but hold it sacred and gladly hear and learn it.

The Word is regarded as sacred because it sanctifies. The Word of God condemns and makes alive. The encounter with preaching and His Word makes us and keeps us Christians, forgives our sins, brings us as guests at the Lord's own table for forgiveness, and sends us off into our manifold vocations joyful, forgiven, and ready to speak the Gospel, serve, and forgive those around us. Only a fool would disagree with King David. "I was glad when they said to me, 'Let us go to the house of the LORD!'" (Psalm 122:1).

WHY AM I JOY:FULLY LUTHERAN?

I know what God's Word is. I know the Scriptures are God's Word. I have a faithful pastor who preaches God's Word.

O Lord, in the Third Commandment, You **instruct** me that I am to take time to tend to preaching and the Word of God. I am to regard it as sacred and gladly hear and learn it.

I **thank** You, dear Lord, that You have given the Church Your perfect written Word and that You have given pastors to preach and teach Your Word. I **thank** You for the privilege of daily meditation on the Holy Scriptures and for regular weekly worship, where I receive Your blessed gifts. I **thank** You that through such gifts You forgive me, strengthen my heart, and make me rejoice.

I **confess** that too often I am sluggish in reading Your Word. I have missed church, failed to give thanks for a faithful congregation and pastor, and failed to give attention to Your Word preached.

Forgive me, O Lord, I pray. Bless my pastor with joy in his task of preaching and teaching. Make me attentive to Your Word, that I "gladly hear and learn it." "I rejoice at Your word like one who finds great spoil" (Psalm 119:162). Amen.

CHAPTER 4

The Fourth Commandment
Honor your father and your mother.

> *What does this mean?* We should fear and love God so that we do not despise or anger our parents and other authorities, but honor them, serve and obey them, love and cherish them.

Let your father and mother be glad; let her who bore you rejoice. **(PROVERBS 23:25)**

The first three commandments define our relationship to God. The next seven define our relationships to other people. "So we have two kinds of fathers presented in this commandment: fathers in blood and fathers in office. Or, those who have the care of the family and those who have the care of the country. Besides these there are still spiritual fathers . . . who govern and guide us by God's Word" (LC I 158).

Fearing and loving God results in honoring parents and authorities. Mistreating the neighbor, or despising legitimate authority, is always a sin against the First Commandment and the Fourth. Jesus repeatedly acknowledged legitimate authority. He castigated the Pharisees for allowing people to fail to care for parents by giving money for religious purposes (Mark 7:9–13). He acknowledged the authority of religious leaders—even though they were corrupt—because they "sit on Moses' seat" (Matthew 23:2). He recognized the authority of the Roman government to strike coinage and tax (Mark 12:17). In dealing with soldiers and centurions, Jesus told no one to quit the military (Luke 7:1–10). Jesus was obedient to His parents as a boy (Luke 2:41–51). And He deeply honored His mother, even while hanging on the cross (John 19:25–27). Jesus kept the commandment perfectly.

Luther called this commandment "the chief and greatest"

commandment of the second table. How much joy and gladness are produced when children love and honor parents! "Children, obey your parents in the Lord, for this is right. 'Honor your father and mother' (this is the first commandment with a promise), 'that it may go well with you and that you may live long in the land'" (Ephesians 6:1–3). How much rejoicing resounds when parents, too, respect this Fourth Commandment and love their children. "Fathers, do not provoke your children to anger, but bring them up in the discipline and instruction of the Lord" (Ephesians 6:4).

How families crumble under harsh parents. How much pain is caused when children fail to love and respect parents. Lives are cursed. Sins are committed. Harsh words are shouted. Deep wounds scar lifetimes. Unhealthy patterns curse generations. Faith in God falters. There is no family prayer at home, no going to church, no speaking of forgiveness. Worry, sleeplessness, disrespect, anger, hatred, fighting, and abuse destroy lives and render them joyless and bitter.

What is born in the home is perpetuated in public life. The shattering of healthy authority and respect at home infects the larger culture with disrespect for the rights of others, flaunting of the law and legal order and authorities. But there are other Fourth Commandment sins that plague all Christians personally.

I chafe at authority, whether at home, in government, or in church. I complain incessantly about elected leaders and rarely pray for them. Teachers stand in the place of parents in the place of God. "To God, to parents, and to teachers we can never offer enough thanks and compensation" (LC I 130). Yet how I have ridiculed them! I make a show of serving my parents, but in my heart, I sin. I often think little of caring for and loving my parents, as though God had so many other much greater and more important things for me to do!

You should be heartily glad and thank God that He has chosen you and made you worthy to do a work so precious and pleasing to Him. Only note this: although this work is regarded as the most humble and despised, consider it great and precious. Do this not because of the worthiness of parents, but because this work is included in, and controlled by, the jewel and sanctuary, namely, the Word and commandment of God. (LC I 117)

Even if I should make a necessary stand against authority used wrongly, I whine and complain about it and express hatred and ill will, instead of doing what the blessed apostles did: "They left the presence of the council, rejoicing that they were counted worthy to suffer dishonor for the name [of Jesus]" (Acts 5:41). O Lord! Have mercy!

WHY AM I JOY:FULLY LUTHERAN?

I am blessed to know that parents and legitimate authorities, including my pastor, are God's own gift for good. I shall receive these gifts with joy. And when I exercise divinely given authority, I shall do so humbly, recognizing that I am God's own servant in doing so.

Dear Lord Christ, You **instruct** me by Your words and actions that I am to honor parents and other authorities.

I **thank** You, Lord, that You have blessed me with loving parents—who are not perfect, to be sure—who have loved me and cared for me the best they knew how. I **thank** You for my pastor and leaders in the church. I **thank** You for all the honorable leaders in the civic realm who have served me, including elected officials, police, and civil servants. I **thank** You for all the joys that have been mine because of these gifts.

I **confess**, Lord, that I have often sinned against legitimate authority in thought, word, and deed. I have disrespected my parents. I have chafed at authority instead of willingly serving and putting the best construction on everything as You Yourself did in Your days living in ancient Israel. I have abused authority in my own exercise of it.

O Lord, forgive me my many sins. "Restore to me the joy of Your salvation" (Psalm 51:12). Grant me joy in loving and serving my family. Give me the strength of body, soul, and faith to love and cherish my parents and other authorities, that I may live a blessed and happy life in my earthly days and be granted eternal life at the end. Amen.

CHAPTER 5

The Fifth Commandment
You shall not murder.

> *What does this mean?* We should fear and love God so that we do not hurt or harm our neighbor in his body, but help and support him in every physical need.

For everything there is a season, and a time for every matter under heaven: . . . a time to kill, and a time to heal . . . a time to weep, and a time to laugh. **(ECCLESIASTES 3:1, 3, 4)**

"God and government are not included in this commandment" (LC I 181). "To punish evil doers, God has delegated His authority to the government, not parents" (LC I 181). "Now," says Luther, "we go forth from our house among our neighbors to learn how we should live with one another" (LC I 180).

. . . so that we do not hurt or harm our neighbor in his body,

At first glance, it seems we can make short shrift of this commandment and move on to the next. I'm no murderer, after all. Not too many people are. It would seem that on the path to joy we might joyfully waltz past this one and on to other real challenges. Not so fast. As with all the Law, God not only expects our hands, feet, and mouths to do and say the right things, but He also expects our thoughts to be sinless. "Be perfect, as your heavenly Father is perfect" (Matthew 5:48).

Jesus Himself does not lighten the burden of this commandment; He increases it exponentially. Jesus lays bare the anger that gives birth to murder.

You have heard that it was said to those of old, "You shall not murder; and whoever murders will be liable to judgment." But I say to you that everyone who is angry with his brother will be liable to judgment; whoever insults his brother will be liable to the council; and whoever says, "You fool!" will be liable to the hell of fire. So if you are offering your gift at the altar and there remember that your brother has something against you, leave your gift there before the altar and go. First be reconciled to your brother, and then come and offer your gift. Come to terms quickly with your accuser while you are going with him to court, lest your accuser hand you over to the judge, and the judge to the guard, and you be put in prison. Truly, I say to you, you will never get out until you have paid the last penny. (Matthew 5:21–26)

The apostle John captured Jesus' thought: "Everyone who hates his brother is a murderer" (1 John 3:15). Luther summarizes Jesus' words above. "He says that we must not kill, neither with hand, heart, mouth, signs, gestures, help, nor counsel. Therefore, this commandment forbids everyone to be angry, except those (as we said) who are in the place of God" (LC I 182).

This commandment does not restrain legitimate punishment by government for heinous crimes (Romans 13:1–4). Nor does this commandment apply to soldiers engaged in just wars.

I have not murdered anyone. But I have hated. According to the exacting standard of the New Testament, I am a murderer. Why do I choose such horrible thoughts of retribution rather than forgiveness and joy? What does my hatred gain? Surely not my brother (Matthew 18). What does it earn me but God's wrath and displeasure?

. . . but help and support him in every physical need.

Yet the positive side of this commandment is all the more damning. I am to "help and support" my neighbor "in every physical need." Truth be told, I'm sluggish in even speaking to my neighbors. I'm often so absorbed with my own woes that I fail to compassionately inquire about the well-being of others. If someone should ask me for a little money for a legitimate need, I feel as though I'm being asked to give away my sacred gods and idols, masking my greed with a show of responsibility and caution.

What shall be said of me at the last trump? "As you did not do it to the least of these, you did not do it to Me" (Matthew 25:45). O Jesus, help! I am curved in on myself and joyless!

You, Jesus, loved the man with the unclean spirits and freed him (Mark 1:25). You healed the sick and oppressed (Mark 1:29–39). You had compassion on lepers, touched and cleansed them (Mark 1:41). You healed the paralytic (Mark 2:3–12). You healed the man with a withered hand (Mark 3:1–5). You healed the man oppressed by a demon (Mark 5:1–20). You healed the woman with the flow of blood (Mark 5:34). You raised Jairus's daughter (Mark 5:42). You fed the five thousand (Mark 6:30–44). You had compassion on the Canaanite woman (Mark 7:24–30), fed the four thousand (Mark 8:1–10), healed the blind man at Bethsaida (Mark 8:22–26), and much more. You, Jesus, loved Your enemies and still do. "Father, forgive them, for they know not what they do" (Luke 23:34). You, O blessed Christ, kept the Fifth Commandment for me.

WHY AM I JOY:FULLY LUTHERAN?

The Fifth Commandment reveals the sinful depths of my selfish heart, accuses me, and slays me. Yet I believe it is Jesus who forgives my sins and resurrects in me the joy of loving and serving others.

Lord Jesus, You **instruct** me by word and deed that I am to refrain from evil thoughts, words, and deeds against my neighbor. And I am to "help and support him in every physical need."

I **thank** You, Jesus, that You call out my sin by Your clear word of Law. I thank You that You give me a glowing example of love for my neighbor in all You did during Your earthly walk.

I **confess** my joyless, petty, constant infractions against this commandment. I **confess** my horrid sins. I have even seethed with hatred toward others, desiring hurt and harm. My thoughts, words, and deeds condemn me.

O Savior of the wretched, healer of the blind, forgive me—a wretched, blind sinner. Heal my cold heart with Your touch, and make me Your own. Give me Your heart of mercy, love, and joyful service. I plead it for Your sake. Amen.

CHAPTER 6

THE SIXTH COMMANDMENT
You shall not commit adultery.

> *What does this mean?* We should fear and love God so that we lead a sexually pure and decent life in what we say and do, and husband and wife love and honor each other.

Let your fountain be blessed, and rejoice in the wife of your youth. **(PROVERBS 5:18)**

. . . so that we lead a sexually pure and decent life in what we say and do,

Of all the things sin has distorted and destroyed, none is more horribly on display in this world than sex and marriage. Outside the bonds of marriage of man and wife, sex as lust distorts life, sends countless people on a lonely quest for pseudosatisfactions, leaves in its wake fatherless children, broken families, pain beyond belief, and the greatest social ills. The Bible condemns unchaste talk. "Let there be no filthiness nor foolish talk nor crude joking, which are out of place, but instead let there be thanksgiving" (Ephesians 5:4). The Bible universally condemns sex outside of marriage. "Or do you not know that the unrighteous will not inherit the kingdom of God? Do not be deceived: neither the sexually immoral, nor idolaters, nor adulterers, nor men who practice homosexuality" (1 Corinthians 6:9).

Our world is filled with the misuse of sex. And our sinful flesh is no help. How can Christians possibly find the strength and aid to live chastely? Jesus. The answer to all sexual sin, whether one is married or unmarried, is Jesus. Repent daily. Avoid opportunities for the flesh. Cling to Jesus in His Word. "No temptation has overtaken you that is not common to man. God is faithful, and He will not let you be tempted beyond your ability, but with the temptation He will also provide the way of escape, that you may be able to endure it" (1 Corinthians 10:13). Christians are not sinless; they are in the struggle against sin (Romans 7).

. . . and husband and wife love and honor each other.

Even after millennia, Adam's joy still leaps from the pages of Genesis. "This at last is bone of my bones and flesh of my flesh; she shall be called Woman, because she was taken out of Man" (Genesis 2:23). There is hardly a gift more glorious and wonderful than male and female. Jesus emphatically affirmed the gift of sex within marriage between a man and a woman.

> Have you not read that He who created them from the beginning made them male and female, and said, "Therefore a man shall leave his father and his mother and hold fast to his wife, and the two shall become one flesh"? So they are no longer two but one flesh. What therefore God has joined together, let not man separate. (Matthew 19:4–6)

"This commandment is aimed directly at the state of marriage. . . . Mark well how gloriously God honors and praises this estate" (LC I 206). God created marriage for a blessed companionship of mutual, sacrificial love. The joy of attraction, affection, courtship, and becoming "one flesh" with one's spouse is undeniable. The apostle Paul forever captured the glorious spirit of a Christian marriage. As Christ is the loving, caring head of the Church and as the Church bows its will to love and serve its Savior (Ephesians 5:23–33), so the wife is to submit to, love, and serve her husband. Paul provides similar and likewise extremely difficult divine instruction for the husband. "As Christ loved the church and gave Himself up for her, that He might sanctify her, having cleansed her by the washing of water with the word, so that He might present the church to Himself in splendor, without spot or wrinkle or any such thing, that she might be holy and without blemish. In the same way husbands should love their wives as their own bodies. He who loves his wife loves himself"

31

(Ephesians 5:25–28). Both husband and wife live to serve the other. Paul's description of God's intent for marriage gives neither license for a domineering tyrant of a husband, nor for a wife's subservience, bowing in fearful trepidation to the whim of such a tyrant. She is a "helper fit for him" (Genesis 2:18). Marriage is a partnership of spiritual equals before God, of sexual, intellectual, and spiritual partners, growing together in love through every joy and sorrow shared.

Marriage is God's gift that those married may live a "sexually pure and decent life in what they say and do." It is the only God-pleasing context for sexual intercourse. Marriage, love, and sex belong together. "For where marital chastity is to be maintained, man and wife must by all means live together in love and harmony" (LC I 219). But how is this possible?

Jesus loves marriage. Every married couple and every young person contemplating marriage should read and reread the account of Jesus' first miracle at the wedding at Cana. Jesus was invited. He went. Such weddings were joyous occasions just like today—but among Jewish people of the day, they lasted a full week! There's no prudishness on Jesus' part. Quite the contrary. It was the steward's job to keep the wine flowing all week long, not too little so the party would wane, and not too much so there would be drunkenness (always condemned in the Bible!). The wine ran out. Jesus' mother suggested they approach Jesus about the problem. The result? He turned water into 150 gallons of wine so good it was said, "You have saved the best for last."

Jesus could hardly have more wonderfully and joyously expressed His support for marriage. We need this support in our marriages today, perhaps more than ever.

Jesus provides wonderful help for marriages. He taught that marriage is God's creating and doing. What "God has joined . . ." (Matthew 19:6). The first promises to Adam and Eve still hold. "Be fruitful and multiply!" (Genesis 1:28). Have kids! "Blessed is the man who fills his quiver with them!" (Psalm 127:5). Contrary to our "cleave and leave" worldview of marriage, God taught that man and woman are to "leave" parents and only then "cleave" to each other.

In the midst of sins against God and spouse, sins against family and children, how can a marriage survive? God has placed His fortress around it in this commandment. Marriage may only be broken by adultery and desertion. How can love and joy grow? Only by regularly hearing God's Word of Law and Gospel, only by the life-giving forgiveness of Christ, only by being forgiven and speaking forgiveness to my spouse. Stay away from church at the peril of your marriage.

What of those not given to marry for whatever reason? Must a joyous life elude them? Jesus, our Savior, lived a chaste and decent life in word and deed. And He did it for us as an example, but especially as one who fulfilled the Law perfectly in our stead. "God sent forth His Son, born of a woman, born under the law, to redeem those who are under the law, so that we might receive adoption as sons" (Galatians 4:4–5). In Jesus, no matter the challenge, is joy.

WHY AM I JOY:FULLY LUTHERAN?

I rejoice that God has given the gift of marriage and the gift of chaste and decent life to those married or unmarried. Even though I fall and sin, I know that Jesus has kept this commandment for me, and in repentance and faith, God sees me only as His perfect and chaste child.

Lord Jesus, You have **instructed** us that God the Father is the author of marriage, and we are to honor marriage in every way. We know from Cana that You love and approve of marriage of man and woman. We know You love children ("Let the little children come to Me" [Mark 10:14]). We know You are pleased when husband and wife lead lives of love and service to each other.

I **thank** You, Lord, for the gift of marriage and for the gift of chaste life in word and deed for all Your children.

I **confess** my horrid sins against You and my spouse. My life is fouled and soiled with sins. I do not honor marriage as I ought and too often fail to love and serve my spouse.

Dear Lord, I have nothing to plead but Your righteous and sinless life, Your sexually pure and decent life in every way. Cover the multitude of my failings. Forgive my sins. Strengthen me for love and service tomorrow. Be present in all Christian marriages and provide for them just as You did at Cana on the blessed day of Your first miracle. Amen.

CHAPTER 7

THE SEVENTH COMMANDMENT
You shall not steal.

What does this mean? We should fear and love God so that we do not take our neighbor's money or possessions, or get them in any dishonest way, but help him to improve and protect his possessions and income.

As sorrowful, yet always rejoicing; as poor, yet making many rich; as having nothing, yet possessing everything. **(2 CORINTHIANS 6:10)**

. . . so that we do not take our neighbor's money or possessions, or get them in any dishonest way,

What and who shall be my god? It is the strangest of joy-robbing distortions that the very things (money and possessions) that God Almighty showers "on the just and unjust" (Matthew 5:45) are made into idols, false gods, by us miserable children of men. Sin and our flesh deceive us into "worship[ing] and serv[ing] the creature rather than the Creator, who is blessed forever" (Romans 1:25). Contentment is elusive no matter how much money one possesses. To whom or what do I look for contentment, security, and joy? God's inerrant Word is abundantly clear:

Do not lay up for yourselves treasures on earth, where moth and rust destroy and where thieves break in and steal, but lay up for yourselves treasures in heaven, where neither moth nor rust destroys and where thieves do not break in and steal. For where your treasure is, there your heart will be also.

The eye is the lamp of the body. So, if your eye is healthy, your whole body will be full of light, but if your eye is bad, your whole body will be full of darkness. If then the light in you is darkness, how great is the darkness!

No one can serve two masters, for either he will hate the one and love the other, or he will be devoted to the one and despise the other. You cannot serve God and money. (Matthew 6:19–24)

If mammon is my god, my treasure, my heart will never be satisfied. If mammon is my god, I will be eying the wealth of others and seeking in a sinful way to lay hold of what is not mine. If mammon is my god, then Christ the Lord cannot be my God. Luther quipped that mammon makes a poor god indeed. It has to be protected, locked up in a chest, and worried about constantly. The very thing my misguided heart puts its hope and trust in shall render me, in the end, hopeless, disillusioned, and joyless. If money is my god, the greatest theft is from God Himself. For then I'll be convinced that my possessions are my doing and at my disposal alone, rather than God's gracious gifts to be used for His glory, the extension of the Gospel, and the well-being of my neighbor.

. . . but help him to improve and protect his possessions and income.

The catechism states the negative—that we are not to "take our neighbor's money or possessions"—and then the positive that we are instead to "help him to improve and protect his possessions and income." The Book of Hebrews states, "Keep your life free from love of money, and be *content* with what you have, for He has said, 'I will never leave you nor forsake you'" (13:5; emphasis added). St. Paul teaches a great deal about money and its use, particularly in the context of his great collection for the poor in Jerusalem (2 Corinthians 8–9). He wrote, "Whoever sows sparingly will also reap sparingly, and whoever sows bountifully will also reap bountifully" (2 Corinthians 9:6). In God's marvelous economy, generosity is richly rewarded. "God loves a cheerful giver. And God is able to make all grace abound to you, so that having all sufficiency in all things at all times, you may abound in every good work" (2 Corinthians 9:7–8).

How can my love of money and possessions be broken? How can I become generous such that I deeply desire to help my neighbor "improve and protect his possessions and income"? Only Jesus.

Only Jesus kept this commandment perfectly. "Foxes have holes, and birds of the air have nests, but the Son of Man has nowhere to lay His head" (Matthew 8:20). Jesus and His disciples kept a cache of money. The money was kept to care for the needs of Jesus and the apostolic band and to provide for the needy (John 12:5). It was the subject of Judas's greed. He succumbed to the god of mammon (John 13:29; 12:6; Matthew 26:15).

Only Jesus not only fulfilled the righteous demands of the Seventh Commandment, but also spent Himself for a wretch like me, who has so miserably transgressed it in thought, word, and deed. "For you know the grace of our Lord Jesus Christ, that though He was rich, yet for your sake He became poor, so that you by His poverty might become rich" (2 Corinthians 8:9). This is St. Paul's strong Christological argument—even more so, the strongest Gospel motivation for Christians not to be controlled by lust for money and possessions and, moreover, to be generous to others.

WHY AM I JOY:FULLY LUTHERAN?

I am Joy:fully Lutheran because I know full well that despite my constant propensity to value money and possessions more than God Himself, Jesus kept the Seventh Commandment perfectly and in my place. Jesus is my God. My heart shall not be ruled by greed. I am free to use money and possessions in service to Christ and my neighbor.

O blessed Jesus, You so clearly **instruct** us that You alone are our God and Savior, our joy and consolation in this life and the next. You tell us, "Do not be anxious about your life, what you will eat or what you will drink, nor about your body. . . . Seek first the kingdom of God and His righteousness, and all these things will be added to you" (Matthew 6:25, 33). The psalm is a millionfold true of You: "He has pity on the weak and the needy, and saves the lives of the needy" (Psalm 72:13).

O most holy and benevolent Christ, what do I have that has not been a gift from You? I thank You for this body and life. I **thank** You for the will to work. I **thank** You for showering blessing upon blessing on me, all undeserved. I **thank** You for my employment. I **thank** You for my parents and others who have cared for me at their own expense. I **thank** You for every penny You have brought to me that all my needs be more than fulfilled. I **thank** You for the need of my neighbor, body and soul, that I have every opportunity to provide for him.

O just Judge and righteous God, I **confess** my theft. I **confess** my greed. I **confess** my insatiable desire for things. I **confess** my jealousy over my neighbor's wealth. I **confess** my thanklessness for Your manifold and endless blessings. I thank You for the promise that as I am generous, You shall provide all I need and even more (Proverbs 19:17).

O gracious Savior, forgive my many sins against this commandment. Give me a clean and renewed conscience. Cause me to recognize Your blessings with joy. Give me a generous heart after Your own. Cause me to be a great blessing to others even as I help and aid them for the well-being of body and soul. When I see injury done to my neighbor, grant me the courage to "interfere and prevent it" (LC I 250). O Lord, may my joy be found only in You. May my joy in giving abound. Finally, all that I may serve You, may I "with a joyful conscience enjoy a hundred times more than [I] could scrape together with unfaithfulness and wrong" (LC I 253). I plead it only for Your sake. Amen.

CHAPTER 8

THE EIGHTH COMMANDMENT
You shall not give false testimony against your neighbor.

What does this mean? We should fear and love God so that we do not tell lies about our neighbor, betray him, slander him, or hurt his reputation, but defend him, speak well of him, and explain everything in the kindest way.

[Love] rejoices with the truth. **(1 CORINTHIANS 13:6)**

The tongue is a small member, yet it boasts of great things. How great a forest is set ablaze by such a small fire! **(JAMES 3:5)**

. . . so that we do not tell lies about our neighbor, betray him, slander him, or hurt his reputation,

The original intent of this commandment had to do with bearing witness in legal proceedings among the ancient people of God. Luther, following St. Augustine, broadens the commandment to include lying in general and dealing with sin and conflict among God's people (Peters, *Ten Commandments*, 287). This is quite in keeping with the New Testament (Matthew 18). There is nothing worse, nothing that squeezes more joy out of life in families, communities, and congregations than conflict. We know that families and churches are to be marked by forgiveness and love. When they are not, lives suffer tremendous angst and emotional disappointment.

Conflict is inevitable among sinners. Nothing is more common than individuals having differing views on a situation, including opposing ideas on why a troubling matter exists, what caused it, what motivations are behind the parties involved, and the like. In such situations, mouths run off in ways that exacerbate the situation and cause even more conflict and damage to individuals, families, and congregations (2 Corinthians 12:20). People who experience such conflicts at church (including pastors' spouses and children, laypeople, and young people) too often are soured on the church altogether. Misuse of the tongue can and does have eternal consequences, make no mistake.

Luther uses four important verbs to define and describe false witness: "tell lies about our neighbor, betray him, slander him, or hurt his reputation."

1. **Tell lies:** Jesus gave one of His strongest rebukes to the religious leaders who wanted to kill Him. They were liars, motivated by the "father of lies," who through lies brought sin into the world. ("But the serpent said to the woman, 'You will not surely die'" [Genesis 3:4]. "You are of your father the devil, and your will is to do your father's desires. He was a murderer from the beginning, and does not stand in the truth, because there is no truth in him. When he lies, he speaks out of his own character, for he is a liar and the father of lies. . . . Whoever is of God hears the words of God. The reason why you do not hear them is that you are not of God" [John 8:44, 47].)

   Lying is very serious business in the New Testament. "If anyone says, 'I love God,' and hates his brother, he is a liar" (1 John 4:20). In fact, liars are consigned to hell. "But as for the cowardly, the faithless, the detestable, as for murderers, the sexually immoral, sorcerers, idolaters, *and all liars*, their portion will be in the lake that burns with fire and sulfur, which is the second death" (Revelation 21:8; emphasis added).

2. **Betray:** This betrayal occurs when I see my neighbor sin and, instead of covering over it (like the sons of Noah covering his drunken nakedness; Genesis 9:23), taking the matter to the proper authority quietly, or speaking personally to the individual, I blab the matter in a loveless way, which only causes harm, "just as swine delight to roll themselves in the dirt and root in it with the snout" (LC I 267). "I can indeed see that my neighbor sins, but I have no command to report it to others" (LC I 266).[2] The sick "joy" I might find in being the "insider" with the "goods" on someone is spiritually lethal.

3. **Slander:** Slander is very similar to betrayal. Slander occurs when I do not bring the matter directly and secretly to the person involved, nor do I quietly alert a responsible third party, but rather go behind the back of the person and speak ill of him or reveal his sin to another for no good purpose (Peters, *Ten Commandments*, 288).

4. **Hurt his reputation:** This sums up the whole endeavor. "The neighbor's 'reputation,' his honor, his right, and his good name are taken away from him" (Peters, *Ten Commandments*, 288).

. . . but defend him, speak well of him, and explain everything in the kindest way.

We are to instead take these positive actions:

1. **Defend him:** "Cover the shortcomings and sins of the neighbor" (Peters, *Ten Commandments*, 289).

2. **Speak well of him:** "We clothe whatever blemishes and infirmities we find in our neighbor and serve and help him to promote his honor" (LC I 288).

---

2   There are "notoriously evil" (LC I 289) sins that require reporting to authorities, and the Large Catechism notes such situations.

3. **Explain everything in the kindest way:** "It is especially an excellent and noble virtue for someone always to explain things for his neighbor's advantage and to put the best construction on all he may hear about his neighbor" (LC I 289).

In short, Jesus' directive is operative. "Whatever you wish that others would do to you, do also to them" (Matthew 7:12; see LC I 286). And finally, the Lord Himself has directed us to take matters of concern *directly to the person involved*. "If your brother sins against you, go and tell him his fault, between you and him alone" (Matthew 18:15).

Jesus spoke the truth without fail, especially before religious and government authorities, to His own detriment. Yet He also beautifully and compassionately covered the sins of the woman caught in adultery. "Let him who is without sin among you be the first to throw a stone at her" (John 8:7). And in His magnificently compassionate words from the cross, He prayed for the very ones who had crucified Him, "Father, forgive them, for they know not what they do" (Luke 23:34). Jesus fulfilled the righteous requirements of this commandment for us.

WHY AM I JOY:FULLY LUTHERAN?

I know the importance and power of words. God's Word condemns and makes alive again. Even words from my paltry mouth can destroy, heal, and protect. God's Word clearly instructs me on how to have positive and even joyous relationships with my family, my neighbors, my fellow Christians, and others. Though I fail, I trust in the grace and forgiveness of the one who said from the cross, "Father, forgive them, for they know not what they do" (Luke 23:34).

Dear Jesus, my Savior and Lord, You so carefully and clearly **instruct** me that if I believe I have been wronged by anyone, I should take the matter directly to that person (Matthew 18). I am not to lie, be a gossip, slander others, or pass along hearsay. I am to handle matters honorably and confidentially, just as I would want others to deal with me.

I **thank** You, Lord, that You have provided such clear teaching so that I know how to avoid and remedy conflict in my home, among my family, in the church, and in my community. You teach me so clearly how to lead a joyful life, with an honorable reputation, while protecting the reputation of others.

O beloved Savior, have mercy on me. So often my lips say what ought not be said. So often I interpret matters in the worst way. I fly into a rage when one sin is committed against me, failing to remember my myriad sins against You. Instead of going directly to a brother or sister to resolve a matter, I seethe, I gossip, I defame, and I explain everything in the worst way. I **confess** that I deserve eternal condemnation.

Merciful God and Lord, You kept this commandment even through Your suffering and death on the cross. You did it for me. I plunge my sins into the deepest depths of Your holy wounds. Forgive me when I fail. "Restore to me the joy of Your salvation, and uphold me with a willing spirit" (Psalm 51:12). Give me the will, the strength of faith, and the courage to defend, speak well of, and explain everything in the kindest way. Amen.

CHAPTER 9

THE NINTH COMMANDMENT
You shall not covet your neighbor's house.

> *What does this mean?* We should fear and love God so that we do not scheme to get our neighbor's inheritance or house, or get it in a way which only appears right, but help and be of service to him in keeping it.

THE TENTH COMMANDMENT
You shall not covet your neighbor's wife, or his manservant or maidservant, his ox or donkey, or anything that belongs to your neighbor.

> *What does this mean?* We should fear and love God so that we do not entice or force away our neighbor's wife, workers, or animals, or turn them against him, but urge them to stay and do their duty.

Delight yourself in the LORD, and He will give you the desires of your heart. **(PSALM 37:4)**

Coveting is the ever-present sin of the human heart, born of the illusion that joy can be found elsewhere than in God Himself and the recognition and use of the plethora of legitimate and lawful gifts of body and soul that He alone provides in this life and life hereafter. Lust is truly the root of evil.

These commandments come full circle. Luther expanded the First Commandment to include false gods and the objects that we often turn into gods. These last two commandments (divided this way since St. Augustine, fourth to fifth centuries) attack the very lust of the heart that creates gods of people and possessions. "Evil desire is the motivation behind all individual sinful acts and brings about death" (Peters, *Ten Commandments*, 310).

The language implying ownership of wives and servants was the reality of the ancient tribal culture of Palestine. Luther knew he faced a different situation. "Manservants and maidservants were not free as now to serve for wages as long as they pleased. Jewish servants were their master's property" (LC I 294). As with all the commandments, he interpreted them in the light of Christ and the New Testament.

Coveting is a killjoy:

> If it is not called stealing and cheating, it is still called coveting your neighbor's property, that is, aiming for a possession of it, luring it away from him without his consent, and being unwilling to see him enjoy what God has granted him. (LC I 307)

There is one case in the Bible that, perhaps more than any other, illustrates the evil of coveting as the source of the breaking of all commandments: David and Bathsheba (2 Samuel 11).

> In the spring of the year, the time when kings go out to battle, David sent Joab, and his servants with him, and all Israel. And they ravaged the Ammonites and besieged Rabbah. But David remained at Jerusalem.

> It happened, late one afternoon, when David arose from his couch and was walking on the roof of the king's house, that he saw from the roof a woman bathing; and the woman was very beautiful. (2 Samuel 11:1–2)

David is filled with lust and moves from the sin of the heart ("Everyone who looks at a woman lustfully has already committed adultery with her in his heart" [Matthew 5:28]) to sins of action.

> And David sent and inquired about the woman. And one said, "Is not this Bathsheba, the daughter of Eliam, the wife of Uriah the Hittite?" So David sent messengers and took her, and she came to him, and he lay with her. (Now she had been purifying herself from her un-

cleanness.) Then she returned to her house. (2 Samuel 11:3–4)

Sinful desire (First, Ninth, Tenth Commandments), not repented of but acted on, threw David into a gross violation of the Sixth Commandment.

And the woman conceived, and she sent and told David, "I am pregnant." (2 Samuel 11:5)

David concocted an evil plan to cover his evil action and acted on it, violating the Fourth Commandment (a misuse of authority) and deceitfully violating the Eighth Commandment (lying).

So David sent word to Joab, "Send me Uriah the Hittite." And Joab sent Uriah to David. When Uriah came to him, David asked how Joab was doing and how the people were doing and how the war was going. Then David said to Uriah, "Go down to your house and wash your feet." And Uriah went out of the king's house, and there followed him a present from the king. But Uriah slept at the door of the king's house with all the servants of his lord, and did not go down to his house. When they told David, "Uriah did not go down to his house," David said to Uriah, "Have you not come from a journey? Why did you not go down to your house?" Uriah said to David, "The ark and Israel and Judah dwell in booths, and my lord Joab and the servants of my lord are camping in the open field. Shall I then go to my house, to eat and to drink and to lie with my wife? As you live, and as your soul lives, I will not do this thing." (2 Samuel 11:6–11)

Uriah, the convert, was far more honorable than the Lord's own anointed prophet and king! David misused God's name (violating the Second Commandment)—acting dishonorably under the guise of his elevated position as the Lord's own leader.

Then David said to Uriah, "Remain here today also, and

tomorrow I will send you back." So Uriah remained in Jerusalem that day and the next. And David invited him, and he ate in his presence and drank, so that he made him drunk. And in the evening he went out to lie on his couch with the servants of his lord, but he did not go down to his house. (2 Samuel 11:12–13)

The first violation of the Fifth Commandment occurs (getting Uriah drunk), and the deceptive action broadens and deepens to premeditated murder (Fifth Commandment), while misusing his authority and involving Joab in the deceptive and murderous plot (Fourth and Eighth Commandments).

In the morning David wrote a letter to Joab and sent it by the hand of Uriah.

In the letter he wrote, "Set Uriah in the forefront of the hardest fighting, and then draw back from him, that he may be struck down, and die." And as Joab was besieging the city, he assigned Uriah to the place where he knew there were valiant men. And the men of the city came out and fought with Joab, and some of the servants of David among the people fell. Uriah the Hittite also died. Then Joab sent and told David all the news about the fighting. And he instructed the messenger, "When you have finished telling all the news about the fighting to the king, then, if the king's anger rises, and if he says to you, 'Why did you go so near the city to fight? Did you not know that they would shoot from the wall? Who killed Abimelech the son of Jerubbesheth? Did not a woman cast an upper millstone on him from the wall, so that he died at Thebez? Why did you go so near the wall?' then you shall say, 'Your servant Uriah the Hittite is dead also.'"

So the messenger went and came and told David all that Joab had sent him to tell. The messenger said to David,

"The men gained an advantage over us and came out against us in the field, but we drove them back to the entrance of the gate. Then the archers shot at your servants from the wall. Some of the king's servants are dead, and your servant Uriah the Hittite is dead also." David said to the messenger, "Thus shall you say to Joab, 'Do not let this matter displease you, for the sword devours now one and now another. Strengthen your attack against the city and overthrow it.' And encourage him." (2 Samuel 11:14–25)

Lust produces sin. David intends to steal (Seventh Commandment). Sin produces more sin. Joab knows he is dealing with a deceitful king and follows suit (Fourth and Eighth Commandments).

When the wife of Uriah heard that Uriah her husband was dead, she lamented over her husband. And when the mourning was over, David sent and brought her to his house, and she became his wife and bore him a son. But the thing that David had done displeased the LORD. (2 Samuel 11:26–27)

Besides causing others to sin, David violated

the First Commandment—committed idolatry and lusted.

the Second Commandment—misused God's name.

the Third Commandment—lived the lie, was unrepentant, and ignored God's Word.

the Fourth Commandment—abused his authority.

the Fifth Commandment—committed premeditated murder.

the Sixth Commandment—sexually lusted, fornicated, and committed adultery.

the Seventh Commandment—stole Bathsheba from
Uriah, along with everything the man had.

the Eighth Commandment—initiated a web of lies.

the Ninth and Tenth Commandments—coveted a woman, enticed her, and fell into gross sins.

These sins ruled David until the prophet Nathan confronted him, "You are the man!" (2 Samuel 12:7). Finally, the king repented and prayed Psalm 51, "a Psalm of David, when Nathan the prophet went to him, after he had gone in to Bathsheba":

Have mercy on me, O God,
according to Your steadfast love;
according to Your abundant mercy
blot out my transgressions.
Wash me thoroughly from my iniquity,
and cleanse me from my sin!

For I know my transgressions,
and my sin is ever before me.
Against You, You only, have I sinned
and done what is evil in Your sight,
so that You may be justified in Your words
and blameless in Your judgment.
Behold, I was brought forth in iniquity,
and in sin did my mother conceive me.
Behold, You delight in truth in the inward being,
and You teach me wisdom in the secret heart.

Purge me with hyssop, and I shall be clean;
wash me, and I shall be whiter than snow.
Let me hear joy and gladness;
let the bones that You have broken rejoice.
Hide Your face from my sins,
and blot out all my iniquities.

Create in me a clean heart, O God,
    and renew a right spirit within me.
Cast me not away from Your presence,
    and take not Your Holy Spirit from me.
Restore to me the joy of Your salvation,
    and uphold me with a willing spirit.

Then I will teach transgressors Your ways,
    and sinners will return to You.
Deliver me from bloodguiltiness, O God,
    O God of my salvation,
    and my tongue will sing aloud of Your righteousness.
O Lord, open my lips,
    and my mouth will declare Your praise.
For You will not delight in sacrifice, or I would give it;
    You will not be pleased with a burnt offering.
The sacrifices of God are a broken spirit;
    a broken and contrite heart, O God, You will not despise.

Do good to Zion in Your good pleasure;
    build up the walls of Jerusalem;
then will You delight in right sacrifices,
    in burnt offerings and whole burnt offerings;
    then bulls will be offered on Your altar.

Why am I Joy:fully Lutheran?

I know my heart is prone to evil. I have no illusions about myself. I want what belongs to others. I know from the story of David that unbridled coveting has the power of unlimited human destruction. It is the ultimate killjoy. In Christ, who coveted only to save sinners ("who, though He was in the form of God, did not count equality with God a thing to be grasped" [Philippians 2:6]), my coveting is forgiven and my eyes are open to rejoice in my blessings.

Dear Lord God, You, my blessed Savior, fulfilled perfectly all the righteous demands of the Ninth and Tenth Commandments; You shunned all "envy and miserable greed" (LC I 310). You **instruct** me by Your Word that desire for what belongs to others is sin. You **instruct** me that I am to treat others as I would have them treat me (Matthew 7:12). You **instruct** me to "put to death therefore what is earthly in [me]: sexual immorality, impurity, passion, evil desire, and covetousness, which is idolatry" (Colossians 3:5).

I **thank** You, Lord Jesus, that You have given me such a clear example of the consequence of covetousness and the horrid spiral of sin in the life of King David. If such a great king and prophet fell so terribly, how vulnerable am I?

I **confess** to You, my God, that I am fully aware of this fire of lust and coveting that burns in my own heart and how dangerous it is. Too often I have indulged it and even allowed it to break into the flames of evil thoughts, words, and deeds. If the great prophet David could not resist lust, O Lord, what of me, horrid worm that I am?

Jesus, drown the fire of lust in me. I am baptized. I am Yours. I cling to Your perfect life. I cling to Your perfect death. I cling to Your perfect satisfaction for all my wretched sins. Grant me repentance when I fail. Strengthen in me only the desire "to gladly wish and leave [for my neighbor] what he has" (LC I 309). Forgive me and take not the joy of Your salvation from me for eternity. Amen.

Go your way. Eat the fat and drink sweet wine and send portions to anyone who has nothing ready, for this day is holy to our Lord. And do not be grieved, for the **joy** of the LORD is your strength.
(NEHEMIAH 8:10; EMPHASIS ADDED)

CHAPTER 10

The Close of the Commandments
What does God say about all these commandments?

> He says, "I, the LORD your God, am a jealous God, punishing the children for the sin of the fathers to the third and fourth generation of those who hate Me, but showing love to a thousand generations of those who love Me and keep My commandments." (Exodus 20:5–6)
>
> *What does this mean?* God threatens to punish all who break these commandments. Therefore, we should fear His wrath and not do anything against them. But He promises grace and every blessing to all who keep these commandments. Therefore, we should also love and trust in Him and gladly do what He commands.

Many are the sorrows of the wicked,
but steadfast love surrounds the one
who trusts in the LORD. **(PSALM 32:10)**

He says, "I, the LORD your God, am a jealous God,

The Lord is not jealous like mere humans are jealous in petty ways. God is jealous in the sense that He won't stand for His people to be worshiping other gods. "For you shall worship no other god, for the LORD, whose name is Jealous, is a jealous God" (Exodus 34:14). Such jealousy is law. "For the LORD your God is a consuming fire, a jealous God" (Deuteronomy 4:24). As the lightning thundered on Sinai when the Lord gave His Ten Commandments to Moses, and any man or beast who touched the mountain would die, so today His Law threatens temporal and eternal punishment and kills. Repent!

. . . punishing the children for the sin of the fathers to the third and fourth generation of those who hate Me,

Faithlessness very often curses generations. It trains a child up in the way he *should not* go (see Proverbs 22:6). How often do we see families who worship gods of other religions, or families who worship other gods in the sense of the idols of money or fame or who are thieves or unfriendly, quarrelsome, unforgiving, and mean or have bitter lives? Though to be sure, non-Christians often seem to relish in all kinds of blessings, a topic of consternation for the psalmists. This is a warning for me. What shall my legacy be in my family? Faith? Or idolatry? Lord, grant me repentance.

. . . but showing love to a thousand generations of those who love Me and keep My commandments." (Exodus 20:5–6)

Here, to love God is to have faith. This is a Gospel promise. People of faith in Christ shun the gods of other religions. "Jesus said to him, 'I am the way, and the truth, and the life. No one comes to the Father except through Me'" (John 14:6). People of faith, forgiven in Christ, fight against making an idol of things or self or sex or power or sinful control over others, though they often fail. "But the fruit of the Spirit is love, joy, peace, patience, kindness, goodness, faithfulness" (Galatians 5:22). The Law of the Lord is a blessed guide for the believer, and the Lord showers His blessings on those who trust in Him and seek (however imperfectly) to follow His Law.

The law of the LORD is perfect,
    reviving the soul;
the testimony of the LORD is sure,
    making wise the simple;
the precepts of the LORD are right,
    rejoicing the heart;
the commandment of the LORD is pure,
    enlightening the eyes;
the fear of the LORD is clean,
    enduring forever;

the rules of the LORD are true,
    and righteous altogether.

More to be desired are they than gold,
    even much fine gold;

sweeter also than honey
    and drippings of the honeycomb.

Moreover, by them is your servant warned;
    in keeping them there is great reward. (Psalm 19:7–11)

What does this mean? God threatens to punish all who break these commandments. Therefore, we should fear His wrath and not do anything against them.

I plead, "Jesus! Savior! Forgive my many sins, and 'renew a right spirit within me' (Psalm 51:10)." "Remember not the sins of my youth or my transgressions; according to Your steadfast love remember me, for the sake of Your goodness, O LORD!" (Psalm 25:7).

But He promises grace and every blessing to all who keep these commandments. Therefore, we should also love and trust in Him and gladly do what He commands.

"For the LORD is righteous; He loves righteous deeds; the upright shall behold His face" (Psalm 11:7).

1. We believe, teach, and confess that the distinction between the Law and the Gospel is to be kept in the Church with great diligence as a particularly brilliant light. By this distinction, according to the admonition of St. Paul, God's Word is rightly divided (see 2 Timothy 2:15).

2. We believe, teach, and confess that the Law is properly a divine doctrine (Romans 7:12). It teaches what is right and pleasing to God, and it rebukes everything that is sin and contrary to God's will.

3. For this reason, then, everything that rebukes sin is, and belongs to, the preaching of the Law.

4. But the Gospel is properly the kind of teaching that shows what a person who has not kept the Law (and is therefore condemned by it) is to believe. It teaches that Christ has paid for and made satisfaction for all sins (see Romans 5:9). Christ has gained and acquired for an individual—without any of his or her own merit—forgiveness of sins, righteousness that avails before God, and eternal life (see Romans 5:10).

> The Gospel comforts consciences against the terrors of the Law, points only to Christ's merit, and raises them up again by the lovely preaching of God's grace and favor, gained through Christ's merit. (FC Ep V 7)

WHY AM I JOY:FULLY LUTHERAN?

Because I know that "the distinction between the Law and the Gospel is a particularly brilliant light. It serves the purpose of rightly dividing God's Word and properly explaining and understanding the Scriptures of the holy prophets and apostles. We must guard this distinction with special care, so that these two doctrines may not be mixed with each other, or a law be made out of the Gospel. When that happens, Christ's merit is hidden and troubled consciences are robbed of comfort" (FC SD V 1).

Holy and righteous God, You **instruct** me that having other gods is a serious mistake and brings Your wrath and condemnation.

Holy and just God, I **thank** You that You have given me this clear instruction for my benefit and for the benefit of my family and the generations that follow.

Holy and righteous God, I **confess** that while I have not believed in the fake and false gods of other religions, I do constantly idolize things that appear to promise joy, peace, security, and hope.

Holy and merciful God, I repent. I trust Your Word. I believe the truth of Your Law and Gospel. Kill my idols. Help me to love Your Law and follow it. Make me a blessing to my children, my family, my community, and my church for the generations that follow me. Amen.

THE CREED

As the head of the family should teach it
in a simple way to his household

CHAPTER 11

THE FIRST ARTICLE
Creation

**I believe in God, the Father Almighty,
Maker of heaven and earth.**

> *What does this mean?* I believe that God has made me and all creatures; that He has given me my body and soul, eyes, ears, and all my members, my reason and all my senses, and still takes care of them.
>
> He also gives me clothing and shoes, food and drink, house and home, wife and children, land, animals, and all I have. He richly and daily provides me with all that I need to support this body and life.
>
> He defends me against all danger and guards and protects me from all evil.
>
> All this He does only out of fatherly, divine goodness and mercy, without any merit or worthiness in me. For all this it is my duty to thank and praise, serve and obey Him.
>
> This is most certainly true.

Let Israel be glad in his Maker; let the children of Zion rejoice in their King! **(PSALM 149:2)**

In the Ten Commandments, "we have seen all that God wants us to do or not to do. Now there properly follows the Creed, which sets forth to us everything that we must expect and receive from God" (LC II 1). The explanation of the First Commandment tells us that we are to "fear, love, and trust in God above all things." But this commandment and the others neither tells us who this God is nor gives us the ability to even begin to keep the Commandments. "All human ability is far too feeble and weak to keep them" (LC II 2). "If we could by our own powers keep the Ten Commandments as they should be kept, we would need nothing further, neither the Creed nor the Lord's Prayer" (LC II 3).

The Creed tells us exactly who God is, what He does, and "how . . . we [can] praise, or show and describe Him, that He may be known" (LC II 10). The First Article teaches us—based squarely on the Bible—that God is our Father, He is almighty, and He is maker of heaven and earth. In six days, He created all things out of nothing (Genesis 1). As we shall note in the Second Article of the Creed, Jesus makes this Father known. Jesus said, "Whoever has seen Me has seen the Father" (John 14:9). There are three articles in the Creed because there are three distinct persons in the one Holy Trinity. Yet there are not three Gods, but only one, Father, Son, and Holy Spirit. "Go therefore and make disciples of all nations baptizing them in the *name* [singular] of the Father and of the Son and of the Holy Spirit" (Matthew 28:19; emphasis added).

Though the Son of God (John 1:3, "All things were made through Him") and the Holy Spirit participated in creation in the beginning (Genesis 1:2) and continue with the Father to sustain all creation (Colossians 1:17), it is God the Father who is called the "Creator of heaven and earth."

***What does this mean?* I believe that God has made me and all creatures; that He has given me my body and soul, eyes, ears, and all my members, my reason and all my senses, and still takes care of them.**

The catechism proceeds from the creation of the believer, the confessor of the Creed. The bedrock of a life of joy is laid here. I know who God is, and I believe He made me. I am His precious creation. God not only knows me and numbers the very hairs of my head (Luke 12:7), but He also has purposefully created me and all creatures. He has made every human being either male or female (Genesis 5:2; Matthew 19:4). He is responsible for my entire body, my reason, and my senses. All these are wondrous and good gifts, already declared "good" at the creation of Adam and Eve. I am to delight in my ability to think, taste, feel, and touch. "I will praise You, for I am fearfully and wonderfully made" (Psalm 139:14). My life is precious to my Creator, and so also is every other human life.

Moreover, God's creation is continuous (Acts 17:28). If He were to withdraw His hand, my life—all life—would collapse.

He also gives me clothing and shoes, food and drink, house and home, wife and children, land, animals, and all I have. He richly and daily provides me with all that I need to support this body and life.

Not only that, but "whatever else is in heaven and upon the earth is daily given, preserved, and kept for us by God" (LC II 19). God's creation provides for all my needs. All mundane necessities—though provided by other creatures, as God's "masks"—are God's own beautiful gifts to me. In fact, I myself can rejoice that I, too, am God's "mask" to provide for the well-being of others and all creatures in the purview of my life. God is at work to serve others through me. "Creatures are only the hands, channels, and means by which God gives all things" (LC I 26).

I am to, and in fact do, find joy in all these creatures. "Let your fountain be blessed, and rejoice in the wife of your youth" (Proverbs 5:18). "Go, eat your bread with joy, and drink your wine with a merry heart, for God has already approved what you do" (Ecclesiastes 9:7). The unending myriad of "First Article gifts" includes vocations, family, relationships, work, hobbies, interests, skills, education, nature, indeed, the whole cosmos. "When the morning stars sang together and all the sons of God shouted for *joy*" (Job 38:7; emphasis added).

He defends me against all danger and guards and protects me from all evil.

I confess in the First Article that God is my Father and He takes care of me. Here the catechism does not elaborate on an otherwise very significant theme in the teaching of Luther, namely, the theology of the cross. That is, like in the case of the very cross of Jesus, God's most loving, caring, and excellent works are hidden by what appears to be the very opposite—namely, suffering, rejection, pain, and death. All of these "work together for good, for those who are called according to His purpose" (Romans 8:28). Indeed, Paul himself bids me to "rejoice in our sufferings, knowing that suffering produces endurance, and endurance produces character, and character produces hope, and hope does not put us to shame, because God's love has been poured into our hearts through the Holy Spirit who has been given to us" (Romans 5:3–5). When suffering comes, I am to confess God as my dear Father in Christ and know that He has purposed all things to work for my eternal good.

Nevertheless, I am to recognize in the daily ebb and flow of my life that God is holding danger at bay, bringing me safely through, and guarding me from evil. If this were not so, I would be overrun at every turn. "Wherever we escape from disaster or danger, we ought to remember that it is God who gives and does all these things. In these escapes we sense and see His fatherly heart and His surpassing love toward us. . . . In this way the heart would be warmed and kindled to be thankful, and to use all such good things to honor and praise God" (LC II 23).

All this He does only out of fatherly, divine goodness and mercy, without any merit or worthiness in me. For all this it is my duty to thank and praise, serve and obey Him.

"If we believed [this article]," says Luther, "[it would] humble and terrify us all. . . . For we sin daily . . . with eyes, ears, hands, body and soul, money and possessions, and everything we have" (LC II 22). God has every cause to abandon me, but wonder of joyous wonders, He does not. Why? All things come to me not because of my worthiness, but only by His goodness and mercy.

"Make a joyful noise to the LORD, all the earth! Serve the LORD with gladness! Come into His presence with singing!

Know that the LORD, He is God! It is He who made us, and we are His" (Psalm 100:1–3). Even more amazingly, God Himself rejoices in us (Proverbs 8:31)!

This is most certainly true.

This conviction is a gift. It comes only from God's Word, knowledge of my sin and need (Romans 7:24), and the divinely wrought recognition that Jesus is my Savior and His Word is true (Romans 8:38–39). "Sanctify them in the truth; Your word is truth" (John 17:17).

WHY AM I JOY:FULLY LUTHERAN?

I know God has made me and all creatures. When I behold the stars of the universe, I marvel with incomprehension at the complexity. Yet, I know the Creator's name: Father, Son, and Holy Spirit. I know that all creation is a precious gift for my good, to be enjoyed in faith. Marvelous.

Almighty Father, Creator of heaven and earth, you **instruct** me in the First Article that I am Your creature. All I am and have (save sin) has been created by You for my good, my pleasure, and my enjoyment and for the service and joy of others.

Holy Father of my Savior, Jesus, I **thank** and praise You that I am Your creation, along with all other blessings in this world and beyond.

I **confess** that even in the face of a million blessings in my person and life, and a billion more in all creation, I use Your creation for sin and evil purpose. I abuse Your creation when I act wrongly toward those You have placed in my life. I complain incessantly; I seethe at times with lust and greed, instead of recognizing the plethora of good You shower on me, Your unworthy creature.

Dear Father, through Your Son's precious passion and

resurrection, forgive me. Wash me. Cleanse me. Absolve me. Renew my heart. Grant me the chaste joy You intend for all Your creation. Widen my heart to acknowledge Your endless kindness, give me a heart after Your own, and grant me joy in You and the blessings of Your gracious hand. Amen.

For You, O LORD, have made me glad by Your work; at the works of Your hands I sing for joy.
(PSALM 92:4)

CHAPTER 12

THE SECOND ARTICLE
Redemption

And in Jesus Christ, His only Son, our Lord, who was conceived by the Holy Spirit, born of the Virgin Mary, suffered under Pontius Pilate, was crucified, died and was buried. He descended into hell. The third day He rose again from the dead. He ascended into heaven and sits at the right hand of God, the Father Almighty. From thence He will come to judge the living and the dead.

What does this mean? I believe that Jesus Christ, true God, begotten of the Father from eternity, and also true man, born of the Virgin Mary, is my Lord,

who has redeemed me, a lost and condemned person, purchased and won me from all sins, from death, and from the power of the devil; not with gold or silver, but with His holy, precious blood and with His innocent suffering and death,

that I may be His own and live under Him in His kingdom and serve Him in everlasting righteousness, innocence, and blessedness,

just as He is risen from the dead, lives and reigns to all eternity.

This is most certainly true.

Then our mouth was filled with laughter, and our tongue with shouts of joy; then they said among the nations, "The LORD has done great things for them." **(PSALM 126:2)**

The faith confessed in the Creed is the faith of the Bible.

I believe in Jesus

"Jesus" is the Greek form of the Hebrew "Jeshua," or "Yahweh Saves." "She will bear a son, and you shall call His name Jesus, for He will save His people from their sins" (Matthew 1:21).

. . . Christ,

This means "Anointed One." God anointed Jesus Redeemer-King (Psalm 2:1–2; Acts 4:25–26). The writer of Hebrews says of Christ, "God . . . has anointed You with the oil of gladness" (Hebrews 1:9). The Christ brings joy to the world (Luke 2:10)!

. . . His only Son,

By faith in Jesus, we are all "sons of God" (Romans 8:14). Jesus, however, by declaring Himself "the Son of God," "was even calling God His own Father, making Himself equal with God" (John 5:18). Jesus is God in the flesh, begotten of the Father in eternity.

. . . our Lord,

"Jesus is Lord" is the earliest confession of the Church. "If you confess with your mouth that Jesus is Lord and believe in your heart that God raised Him from the dead, you will be saved" (Romans 10:9). Paul bases this teaching on Joel 2:32, "Everyone who calls on the name of the LORD [Yahweh!] shall be saved." Jesus is Yahweh in the flesh.

. . . who was conceived by the Holy Spirit,

"Mary said to the angel, 'How will this be, since I am a *virgin*?' And the angel answered her, 'The Holy Spirit will come upon you, and the power of the Most High will overshadow you; therefore the child to be born will be called holy—the Son of God'" (Luke 1:34–35; emphasis added).

. . . born of the Virgin Mary,

"And she gave birth to her firstborn son and wrapped Him in swaddling clothes and laid Him in a manger, because there was no place for them in the inn" (Luke 2:7).

. . . suffered under Pontius Pilate,

"So he [Pilate] delivered Him over to them to be crucified" (John 19:16a).

. . . was crucified,

"So they took Jesus, and He went out, bearing His own cross, to the place called The Place of a Skull, which in Aramaic is called Golgotha. There they crucified Him" (John 19:16b–18).

. . . died

"When Jesus had received the sour wine, He said, 'It is finished,' and He bowed His head and gave up His spirit" (John 19:30).

. . . and was buried.

"So because of the Jewish day of Preparation, since the tomb was close at hand, they laid Jesus there" (John 19:42).

He descended into hell.

"For Christ also suffered once for sins, the righteous for the unrighteous, that He might bring us to God, being put to death in the flesh but made alive in the spirit, in which He went and proclaimed to the spirits in prison" (1 Peter 3:18–19).

The third day He rose again from the dead.

"He was delivered over to death for our sins and was raised to life for our justification" (Romans 4:25 NIV).

He ascended into heaven and sits at the right hand of God, the Father Almighty.

"When He had said these things, as they were looking on, He was lifted up, and a cloud took Him out of their sight" (Acts 1:9). "Jesus Christ . . . has gone into heaven and is at the right hand of God, with angels, authorities, and powers having been subjected to Him" (1 Peter 3:21–22).

From thence He will come to judge the living and the dead.

"Then will appear in heaven the sign of the Son of Man, and then all the tribes of the earth will mourn, and they will see the Son of Man coming on the clouds of heaven with power and great glory" (Matthew 24:30).

What does this mean? I believe that Jesus Christ, true God, begotten of the Father from eternity, and also true man, born of the Virgin Mary, is my Lord,

This is scandalous. The ancients were aghast at the assertion that God should become flesh. The apostle John relished putting Jesus' humanity in starkest terms. "The Word became flesh and dwelt among us" (John 1:14). Luther put the necessity of Christ being both God and man in a striking way:

> We Christians should know that if God is not in the scale to give it weight, we, on our side, sink to the ground. I mean it this way: if it cannot be said that God died for us, but only a man, we are lost; but if God's death and a dead God lie in the balance, His side goes down and ours goes up like a light and empty scale. (SD VIII 44)

This God-man Christ is my Lord. Today when many Christians state, "Jesus is Lord," they have the Law in view. "Jesus is your Savior, but have you made Him your Lord?" (i.e., by obedience). The Bible's confession is quite different. As noted above, the New Testament confession "Jesus is Lord" (Romans 10:9) is a confession that Jesus is Yahweh, God in the flesh. Thomas confessed to the resurrected Christ, "My Lord and my God!" (John 20:28). Luther understands this confession especially in terms of the Gospel.

> "But what does it mean to become Lord?" "It is this. He has redeemed me from sin, from the devil, from death, and from all evil. For before I did not have a Lord or King, but was captive under the devil's power, condemned to death, stuck in sin and blindness." (LC II 27)

who has redeemed me, a lost and condemned person, purchased and won me from all sins, from death, and from the power of the devil; not with gold or silver, but with His holy, precious blood and with His innocent suffering and death,

This is the heart of what Hermann Sasse called the most beautiful paragraph ever composed in the German language. Christ has "redeemed me." To *redeem* is to "buy back" (Leviticus 25:48). Faith says, "Christ has paid the price for *me*." "The life I now live in the flesh I live by faith in the Son of God, who loved *me* and gave Himself *for me*" (Galatians 2:20; emphasis added).

. . . a lost and condemned person,

"And you were dead in the trespasses and sins in which you once walked . . . and were by nature children of wrath, like the rest of mankind" (Ephesians 2:1–3).

. . . purchased and won me from all sins,

"You were bought with a price" (1 Corinthians 7:23).

. . . from death, and from the power of the devil;

"Since therefore the children share in flesh and blood, He Himself likewise partook of the same things, that through death He might destroy the one who has the power of death, that is, the devil" (Hebrews 2:14).

. . . not with gold or silver,

"You were ransomed from the futile ways inherited from your forefathers, not with perishable things such as silver or gold" (1 Peter 1:18).

. . . but with His holy, precious blood

"But with the precious blood of Christ, like that of a lamb without blemish or spot" (1 Peter 1:19). "The *blood of* Jesus His Son cleanses us from all sin" (1 John 1:7; emphasis added).

. . . and with His innocent suffering and death,

"Now when the centurion saw what had taken place, he praised God, saying, 'Certainly this man was innocent!'" (Luke 23:47). "For our sake He made Him to be sin who knew no sin, so that in Him we might become the righteousness of God" (2 Corinthians 5:21).

. . . that I may be His own

"You are Christ's, and Christ is God's" (1 Corinthians 3:23).

. . . and live under Him in His kingdom

"For in this way there will be richly provided for you an entrance into the eternal kingdom of our Lord and Savior Jesus Christ" (2 Peter 1:11).

. . . and serve Him

"[Christ] gave Himself for us to redeem us from all lawlessness and to purify for Himself a people for His own possession who are zealous for good works" (Titus 2:14).

. . . in everlasting righteousness,

"For His sake I have suffered the loss of all things and count them as rubbish, in order that I may gain Christ and be found in Him, not having a righteousness of my own that comes from the law, but that which comes through faith in Christ, the righteousness from God that depends on faith" (Philippians 3:8–9).

. . . innocence,

"Who can discern his errors? Declare me innocent from hidden faults" (Psalm 19:12).

. . . and blessedness,

"Then the King will say to those on His right, 'Come, you who are blessed by My Father, inherit the kingdom prepared for you from the foundation of the world'" (Matthew 25:34).

. . . just as He is risen from the dead,

"But in fact Christ has been raised from the dead, the firstfruits of those who have fallen asleep. For as by a man came death, by a man has come also the resurrection of the dead" (1 Corinthians 15:20–21).

. . . lives and reigns to all eternity.

"And being found in human form, He humbled Himself by becoming obedient to the point of death, even death on a cross. Therefore God has highly exalted Him and bestowed on Him the name that is above every name, so that at the name of Jesus every knee should bow, in heaven and on earth and under the earth, and every tongue confess that Jesus Christ is Lord, to the glory of God the Father" (Philippians 2:8–11).

This is most certainly true.

"Jesus said to the Jews who had believed Him, 'If you abide in My word, you are truly My disciples, and you will know the truth, and the truth will set you free'" (John 8:31–32).

Luther sums up the joyous ramification of this article: "Yes, the entire Gospel that we preach is based on this point, that we properly understand this article as that upon which our salvation and all our *happiness* rests. It is so rich and complete that we can never learn it fully" (LC II 33; emphasis added).

WHY AM I JOY:FULLY LUTHERAN?

I know Jesus. I know and believe that His life—from His preincarnate state as the Word, eternal Son of the Father, to His conception and birth and through to His death, resurrection, ascension, and return on the Last Day—is a Gospel gift for me. Comfort. Consolation. Joy.

O Eternal Word, You **instruct** me in the Creed that from conception to resurrection and into eternity, You assumed my flesh. You became everything that I am, only without sin. You assumed; You redeemed.

Blessed Christ, God and Redeemer, I **confess** You are my Lord. Your blessed Word is rich and full and clear. That Word **instructs** me that You took on flesh in the Virgin's womb. You lived, suffered, died, and rose again for sinners, of which, I confess, I am chief (1 Timothy 1:15).

I **thank** You, blessed Redeemer, that You have paid the price for me and for the world. I thank You for the Creed and all its glorious biblical truth. I **thank** You for Dr. Luther's wonderful explanation and that You have redeemed me, not with silver or gold, but with Your holy and precious blood and Your innocent suffering and death.

I **confess**, gracious Jesus, that I have too often ignored your Word. I have failed to contemplate the depth of Your compassion, the depth of Your Father's love in sending You to bear my sin and be my Savior. I have failed to meditate on and rejoice in the profound gift of Your incarnation and that You became like me in every way, save sin. I have doubted. I sin. I fail to live joyously as Your servant in righteousness, innocence, and blessedness.

Forgive me, divine Redeemer! All this You have done for sinners. I am a sinner. You have done it for me. You are my only hope for time and eternity. Amen.

And the ransomed of the LORD shall return and come to Zion with singing; everlasting joy shall be upon their heads; they shall obtain gladness and joy, and sorrow and sighing shall flee away.
(ISAIAH 35:10)

CHAPTER 13

The Third Article
Sanctification

I believe in the Holy Spirit, the holy Christian church, the communion of saints, the forgiveness of sins, the resurrection of the body, and the life everlasting. Amen.

> *What does this mean?* I believe that I cannot by my own reason or strength believe in Jesus Christ, my Lord, or come to Him; but the Holy Spirit has called me by the Gospel, enlightened me with His gifts, sanctified and kept me in the true faith.
>
> In the same way He calls, gathers, enlightens, and sanctifies the whole Christian church on earth, and keeps it with Jesus Christ in the one true faith.
>
> In this Christian church He daily and richly forgives all my sins and the sins of all believers.
>
> On the Last Day He will raise me and all the dead, and give eternal life to me and all believers in Christ.
>
> This is most certainly true.

May the God of hope fill you with all joy and peace in believing, so that by the power of the Holy Spirit you may abound in hope. **(ROMANS 15:13)**

When I confess, "**I believe in the Holy Spirit**," I am confessing the Third Person of the Holy Trinity is God. When Ananias famously and deceptively deceived the early Christian community,

> Peter said, "Ananias, why has Satan filled your heart to *lie to the Holy Spirit* and to keep back for yourself part of the proceeds of the land? While it remained unsold,

did it not remain your own? And after it was sold, was it not at your disposal? Why is it that you have contrived this deed in your heart? *You have not lied to man but to God.*" (Acts 5:3–4; emphasis added)

The Spirit is called "Holy" because He "makes me holy, as His name implies" (LC II 40). Thus this Third Article is called "sanctification." "Sanctifying is just bringing us to Christ so we receive this good, which we could not get ourselves" (LC II 39).

The work of acquiring all that we need for life in Christ now and into eternity is done. It happened almost two thousand years ago at a place called Golgotha. We cannot, however, go back in time. Even if we could, it would do us no good. We can go to the place in modern Jerusalem where the events of Christ's cross happened, but we have no command in the Bible to do so, nor any promises that in doing so we should find forgiveness. The Creed proceeds to direct us to the place where the benefits of the cross are delivered today.

Those benefits are found in "**the holy Christian church, the communion of saints**." "The Spirit has His own congregation in the world, which is the mother that conceives and bears every Christian through God's Word" (LC II 42). The Large Catechism says that "the communion of saints" is identical in meaning to the "Church." Werner Elert, by an in-depth study of the earliest origins of the words of the Creed, was convinced that "communion of saints" originally referred not to people but rather to the Sacrament and was rendered as "participation in the holy things," namely, the elements of body and blood. The Church is present where the Word, Baptism, and Supper are present. Because faith is hidden, so is the Church. It must be believed even as it is hidden beneath division, sinners, and even heresy and heretics.

The sanctifying happens first by "**the forgiveness of sins**." "Receive the Holy Spirit. If you forgive the sins of any, they are forgiven them; if you withhold forgiveness from any, it is withheld" (John 20:22–23).

The sanctifying begun in this life by Baptism shall mature at the last into "**the resurrection of the body**," my body. As we shall see when we treat Baptism, my Baptism connects me with Christ and all His benefits, including His bodily resurrection (Romans 6:1–11; Colossians 2:12). "For the Lord Himself will descend from heaven with a cry of command, with the voice of an archangel, and with the sound of the trumpet of God. And the dead in Christ will rise first" (1 Thessalonians 4:16).

The resurrection of the body shall immediately precede "**the life everlasting**." Those trusting in Christ who die prior to the resurrection at the Last Day enjoy the blissful presence of Christ until that day (Luke 23:43) and a physical eternity in a "new heaven and earth," a new Eden (2 Peter 3:13). Those who do not know Christ face eternal living death (Matthew 8:12; Revelation 20:15).

What does this mean? **I believe that I cannot by my own reason or strength believe in Jesus Christ, my Lord, or come to Him; but the Holy Spirit has called me by the Gospel, enlightened me with His gifts, sanctified and kept me in the true faith.**

I cannot . . . believe in Jesus,

This phrase, scandalous to every fiber of my human capacity and pride, is the razor that cuts sharply and surely between the religion of Jesus—the religion of grace—and all of its caricature. Faith as my "free decision" is not only a myth, it is an arrogant mixing of Law and Gospel. "Jesus has done everything He could for you. Now it's up to you." Jesus and the Bible teach something inscrutably radical. What Jesus said to His apostles holds for me. "*You did not choose Me*, but *I chose you* and appointed you that you should go and bear fruit and that your fruit should abide" (John 15:16; emphasis added). Paul elucidates this truth so profoundly he must be quoted at some length.

And you were *dead in the trespasses and sins* in which you once walked, following the course of this world, following the prince of the power of the air, the spirit that is now at work in the sons of disobedience—among whom we all once lived in the passions of our flesh, carrying out the desires of the body and the mind, and were *by nature children of wrath, like the rest of mankind.* But God, being rich in *mercy*, because of the great love with which He loved us, *even when we were dead in our trespasses, made us alive together with Christ—by grace* you have been saved—and raised us up with Him and seated us with Him in the heavenly places in Christ Jesus, so that in the coming ages He might show the *immeasurable riches of His grace* in kindness toward us in Christ Jesus. *For by grace you have been saved through faith. And this is not your own doing; it is the gift of God*, not a result of works, so that no one may boast. For we are His workmanship, created in Christ Jesus for good works, which God prepared beforehand, that we should walk in them. (Ephesians 2:1–10)

Dead people don't "decide for Jesus." "Faith comes from hearing, and hearing through the word of Christ" (Romans 10:17). Jesus has decided for me and in time brought me to faith, and the greatest joy in it all is that He shall keep me as His own to eternity. "I give them eternal life, and they will never perish, and no one will snatch them out of My hand" (John 10:28).

When people are called to "choose this day whom you will serve" (Joshua 24:15) or told, "*Behold, I stand at the door and knock.* If anyone hears My voice and opens the door, I will come in to him" (Revelation 3:20), these things are spoken to Christians, who are being urged to continue in the faith, to hold to Christ, to go to church, to be diligent in the Word.

In the same way He calls, gathers, enlightens, and sanctifies the whole Christian church on earth, and keeps it with Jesus Christ in the one true faith.

The whole Christian Church on earth is called. "You . . . are called to belong to Jesus Christ" (Romans 1:6). "Fear not, for I have redeemed you; I have called you by name, you are Mine" (Isaiah 43:1). The Church is tenderly gathered. "He will tend His flock like a shepherd; He will gather the lambs in His arms" (Isaiah 40:11). The Church is enlightened. "The God of our Lord Jesus Christ, the Father of glory, . . . give you the Spirit of wisdom and of revelation in the knowledge of Him, having the eyes of your hearts enlightened, that you may know what is the hope to which He has called you" (Ephesians 1:17–18). The Church is sanctified. "We have been sanctified through the offering of the body of Jesus Christ once for all" (Hebrews 10:10). The Church is kept with Jesus Christ. "In Him you also, when you heard the word of truth, the gospel of your salvation, and believed in Him, were *sealed with the promised Holy Spirit*, who is *the guarantee of our inheritance* until we acquire possession of it, to the praise of His glory" (Ephesians 1:13–14; emphasis added). How Joy:fully comforting that God is the actor in all of this. It's all grace. It's all gift. I am the receiver, along with the whole Church.

. . . in the one true faith.

Jesus is all about the truth. "For I have given them the words that You [Father] gave Me, and they have received them and have *come to know in truth* that I came from You; and they have believed that You sent Me" (John 17:8; emphasis added). There is a constant dividing line in the New Testament between belief that is true and salutary and belief that is false and harmful. "To them we did not yield in submission even for a moment, so that the truth of the gospel might be preserved for you" (Galatians 2:5). The church is "a pillar and buttress of the truth" (1 Timothy 3:15) so far as it holds to God's infallible Word. The Small Catechism confesses the basic truth of Jesus. It's really quite simple. Eternal life is found in the truth of the blessed Gospel of free forgiveness in Jesus' cross and resurrection. If only enough of the Word of Christ and the Sacraments are present and believed, there is the Church, there are believers. Error is dangerous, but mercifully, if only the foundation, Christ, is not overthrown, one may remain a Christian. This is St. Paul's clear and joyful teaching.

For no one can lay a foundation other than that which is laid, which is Jesus Christ. Now if anyone builds on the foundation with gold, silver, precious stones, wood, hay, straw—each one's work will become manifest, for the Day will disclose it, because it will be revealed by fire, and the fire will test what sort of work each one has done. If the work that anyone has built on the foundation survives, he will receive a reward. If anyone's work is burned up, he will suffer loss, though he himself will be saved, but only as through fire. (1 Corinthians 3:11–15)

In this Christian church He daily and richly forgives all my sins and the sins of all believers.

"Everything, therefore, in the Christian Church is ordered toward this goal: we shall daily receive in the Church nothing but the forgiveness of sin" (LC II 55). "Outside of this Christian Church, where the Gospel is not found, there is no forgiveness, as also there can be no holiness" (LC II 56). This forgiveness is "to comfort and encourage our consciences as long as we live here" (LC II 55). I am a rugged individualist. I seek religion that is between God (no matter how I conceive of Him, whether based on the truth of the Bible and Jesus' Word or not) and me. Such religion does not free the conscience. The Bible and catechism teach a Church of believers gathered, the Body of Christ. "So we, though many, are one *body* in *Christ*, and individually members one of another" (Romans 12:5; emphasis added). "For we are in the Christian Church, where there is nothing but ‹continuous, uninterrupted› forgiveness of sin. This is because God forgives us and because we forgive, bear with, and help one another" (LC II 55). The word of the Gospel forgives sins. It does what it says. "The gospel . . . is the power of God for salvation to everyone who believes" (Romans 1:16). Baptism forgives. "Repent and be *baptized* every one of you in the name of Jesus Christ for the forgiveness of your sins" (Acts 2:38; emphasis added). Absolution forgives. "If you forgive the sins of any, they are forgiven them; if you withhold forgiveness from any, it is withheld" (John 20:23). The Lord's Supper delivers forgiveness. "And He took a cup, . . . saying, 'Drink of it, all of you, for this is My blood of the covenant, which is poured out for many for the forgiveness of sins" (Matthew 26:27–28).

All proclamation, whether by pastors publicly or by spiritual priests (all Christians) in their daily vocations or by missionaries sent to lonely outposts to create and gather believers, is the work of God through His Church.

WHY AM I JOY:FULLY LUTHERAN?

I am Joy:fully Lutheran because the Holy Spirit has made me holy, justified me, and preserves me unto eternal life. And this He has done through His Holy Christian Church, by His Word in various ways, and at the hands of pastors. I have "the forgiveness of sins" and "the life everlasting," and I shall be raised up on the Last Day.

O Holy Spirit, sanctify me in the truth, for Your Word is truth. You have **instructed** me with crystal clarity that apart from You I am dead in trespasses and sins. It is Your sanctifying work, through the Church, to create faith in Jesus, to sustain my faith, to forgive my sins, to place me in the Church, to continue daily through Word and Sacrament to forgive my sins and cleanse my conscience. Because we are "for now . . . only half pure and holy" (LC II 58)—having our sins forgiven but daily sinning much—You continuously strengthen and make me holy to live for You by serving my neighbor.

I **thank** You, blessed Spirit, that You speak clearly in Your Word, that I know all things necessary for my temporal living as a Christian and for eternity with You in a resurrected paradise.

I **confess** to You, my God, that in spite of the blessings of faith and forgiveness delivered me, I daily sin much and deserve nothing but punishment.

I pray, O blessed Spirit of Christ and the Father, that You preserve me and all believers in Your Church until the Last Day and that You continue to call, gather, enlighten, and sanctify many more by Your blessed Gospel, until the day of our Lord Jesus Christ, when You shall raise up me and all believers in Christ and take us to be with You forever, even as You live and reign to all eternity. Amen.

THE LORD'S PRAYER

As the head of the family should teach it
in a simple way to his household

CHAPTER 14

Preface

Our Father, who art in heaven, hallowed be Thy name, Thy kingdom come, Thy will be done on earth as it is in heaven. Give us this day our daily bread; and forgive us our trespasses as we forgive those who trespass against us; and lead us not into temptation, but deliver us from evil. For Thine is the kingdom and the power and the glory forever and ever. Amen.

May we shout for joy over your salvation, and in
the name of our God set up our banners!
May the LORD fulfill all your petitions! **(PSALM 20:5)**

"We have now heard what we must do and believe [i.e., in the Ten Commandments and the Creed], in what things the best and happiest life consists. Now follows the third part, how we ought to pray" (LC III 1). The Lord's Prayer is a tremendous source of joy and confidence for Christians. It also provides an opportunity (which Dr. Luther deftly explained for us in the Large Catechism) to teach us about prayer in general and exactly why prayer is a source of solid consolation. The Large Catechism makes five very significant points about prayer (see Peters, *Lord's Prayer*, 7).

1. Prayer has God's command. The Second Commandment forbids the taking of God's name in vain and mandates prayer, praise, and thanksgiving. Prayer is a "duty and obligation" (LC III 8), just like obeying parents or the command not to steal. God wants Christians to pray and commands us to do so. "Pray without ceasing" (1 Thessalonians 5:17). Jesus Himself is our example (see Mark 1:35). Jesus Himself gave us a model prayer in the Lord's Prayer ("Pray then like this" [Matthew 6:9]). We can be confident and joyful in prayer because we know God Himself wants us to pray and Jesus teaches us how.

2. God attaches promises to prayer. "Call upon Me in the day of trouble; I will deliver you" (Psalm 50:15). "Ask, and it will be given to you. . . . For everyone who asks receives" (Matthew 7:7, 8; see LC III 19). "Such promises certainly ought to encourage and kindle our hearts to pray with pleasure and delight. For He testifies with His own Word that our prayer is heartily pleasing to Him. Furthermore, it shall certainly be heard and granted" (LC III 20).

3. In the Lord's Prayer, God Himself puts on our lips the very words we are to pray (LC III 22). There is no way we can doubt that such prayer is pleasing to Him or won't be heard by Him! "God loves to hear it. We ought not to surrender this for all the riches of the world" (LC III 23).

4. The Lord's Prayer helps us recognize our basic needs and to present these needs to our heavenly Father.

5. Prayer is "all our shelter and protection" (LC III 30). It is defensive. "The prayer of a few godly people standing in the middle [is] like an iron wall for our side" (LC III 31). And it is offensive. For when Christians pray "Thy will be done," God responds, "Yes, it shall be" (see LC III 32).

The Lord's Prayer contains "in seven successive articles, or petitions, every need that never ceases to apply to us. Each is so great that it ought to drive us to keep praying the Lord's Prayer all our lives" (LC III 34).

Why am I Joy:fully Lutheran?

I admit, there are times when I feel so oppressed and confused I hardly know what or how to pray. Even then "the Spirit Himself intercedes" (Romans 8:26) and helps me. But I do not wander aimlessly in prayer, wondering whom to pray to and for what to pray. In the Lord's Prayer, Jesus has given me an anchor of certainty. I am invited to pray and to pray with complete confidence that God hears and answers my prayers. I rejoice.

Jesus, my Redeemer, my source of all consolation and joy, You not only prayed daily, but You even prayed in the hours of Your temptation by the devil and in the Garden of Gethsemane. You prayed from the cross. You **instructed** by example, and You taught Your Church to pray, giving us the very words of the Lord's Prayer, which in seven simple petitions encompasses all our needs.

I **thank** You, Lord Jesus, that when I pray the Lord's Prayer, when I pray and meditate on my need and the need of the Church and all people with the words of the Lord's Prayer, I know You hear me. I know You hear the Church. For so You have commanded us to pray and promised to hear us.

I **confess**, Lord, that I have never prayed a perfect Lord's Prayer. My mind wanders incessantly. Despite Your command and promise, I am sluggish in prayer, slow to pray for others, content to wake and lay down again without so much as a single petition to You. Lord, I confess that I am worthy only to have You shut Your ears to my requests.

O Jesus, look not on my failing and faltering attempts at prayer. Hear me for the sake of Your promises. Hear me for the sake of those for whom I pray. Kindle in my heart a greater love and confidence in prayer. Let me and Your whole Church find increasing joy and confidence in presenting our needs before You. Hear my prayer. Thwart the devil and my sinful flesh. Grant me strength of body and soul to be Your prayer warrior, remembering in prayer my need and the needs of all. Amen.

CHAPTER 15

The Introduction
Our Father who art in heaven.

What does this mean? With these words God tenderly invites us to believe that He is our true Father and that we are His true children, so that with all boldness and confidence we may ask Him as dear children ask their dear father.

For you did not receive the spirit of slavery to fall back into fear, but you have received the Spirit of adoption as sons, by whom we cry, "Abba! Father!"
(ROMANS 8:15)

What does this mean? With these words God tenderly invites us

Jesus reveals the tender heart of God the Father toward us. What the prophet promised came true in Jesus. "The LORD your God is in your midst, a mighty one who will save; He will rejoice over you with gladness" (Zephaniah 3:17). Zechariah revealed the task of John the Baptizer, the last and greatest prophet, to reveal the "tender mercy" of the Father in Jesus:

And you, child, will be called the prophet of the Most High; for you will go before the Lord to prepare His ways, to give knowledge of salvation to His people in the forgiveness of their sins, because of the tender mercy of our God. (Luke 1:76–78)

The apostle John tells us, "No one has ever seen God; the only God, who is at the Father's side, He has made Him known" (John 1:18). This God-man, Jesus, tenderly invites us, "Come to Me, all who labor and are heavy laden, and I will give you rest" (Matthew 11:28). Jesus tenderly teaches us to pray like He does, "Our Father."

. . . to believe that He is our true Father and that we are His true children,

Jesus, who verified His authority to speak for the Father by His sinless life, death, and resurrection, invites us to believe. He says to us here, "Believe it. You have a dear Father in heaven who truly loves you. I'm proof of it." There's not much that is more horrifying and damaging than a father who fails to love and care for his own child. A son who rejects his loving father is almost as horrifying. The unconditional love of father and child is perhaps the most powerful human quality for a joyous life, come what may. Infinitely more significant—and eternal—is God the Father's love for each child of His creation. In Jesus, I am invited to believe and acknowledge that the Father of Jesus is my Father. He loves me so much that He did not spare His only begotten Son but gave Him up for me. I am His true child. "See what kind of love the Father has given to us, that we should be called children of God; and so we are" (1 John 3:1).

. . . so that with all boldness and confidence we may ask Him as dear children ask their dear father.

"Through Him [Christ] we . . . have access in one Spirit to the Father. So then you are no longer strangers and aliens, but . . . members of the household of God" (Ephesians 2:18–19). Baptized, clothed with the righteousness of Jesus (Galatians 3:27), invited by Jesus Himself in the Lord's Prayer, we are to be bold and confident when we present our prayers to God. In my service to the Church, I've had access to presidents, senators, and the highest church leaders around the world. All of that is nothing compared to the blessed and joyous privilege of the simplest and most humble Christian to stand before the throne of grace and pray in the name of Jesus, as a dear child of His heavenly Father.

Heavenly Father, almighty and everlasting God, through Your Son You have **instructed** me that because of Jesus, You are my Father in heaven. Jesus has revealed You to be a tender and loving God. It gives You great joy to love Your children and provide for them. It gives You great joy when Your children come to You in prayer, humbly beseeching You to provide for their needs and the needs of others. Wretch that I am, it is unfathomable that I should dare to request anything of You. Yet still more unfathomable is it that it delights You when I come before You boldly and confidently in the name of Jesus.

Why am I Joy:fully Lutheran?

Because God the Father, through Jesus Christ, is my tender, loving Father who loves it when I pray.

Dearest Father, You **instruct** me that I am to approach You in prayer with all boldness and confidence.

I **thank** You that You have shown Yourself to be a Father who rejoices in Your children, even me, worm that I am, and that You love it when I pray.

I **confess** that though I have constant access to Your ear, though I have the clear promise that You hear, though I am commanded to pray and have Your promise that You will provide what's best for me and all that I need, I am sluggish in prayer. I fail to pray for my own needs. I fail to pray for my loved ones. I fail to pray for the Church. I fail to pray for the extension of Your kingdom. I doubt Your benevolence. I question Your will. I live joylessly and fail to give thanks for Your unending gifts, blessings, and answered prayers. I deserve to be cast from Your presence now and eternally.

Gracious Father, forgive me. Plunge my sins into the wounds of Your crucified Son. Strengthen my faith. Give me new resolve to pray. Cause me to rejoice in Your blessings. Grant me a willing, bold, joyous, and confident heart, constantly in prayer for all things pleasing to You, through Jesus Christ, Your Son, our Lord, who lives and reigns with You, now and ever. Amen.

CHAPTER 16

The First Petition
Hallowed be Thy name.

What does this mean? God's name is certainly holy in itself, but we pray in this petition that it may be kept holy among us also.

How is God's name kept holy? God's name is kept holy when the Word of God is taught in its truth and purity, and we, as the children of God, also lead holy lives according to it. Help us to do this, dear Father in heaven! But anyone who teaches or lives contrary to God's Word profanes the name of God among us. Protect us from this, heavenly Father!

For thus says the One who is high and lifted up, who inhabits eternity, whose name is Holy: "I dwell in the high and holy place, and also with him who is of a contrite and lowly spirit." **(ISAIAH 57:15)**

God's name is certainly holy in itself,

King Solomon built the temple and prayed,

But will God indeed dwell on the earth? Behold, heaven and the highest heaven cannot contain You; how much less this house that I have built! Yet have regard to the prayer of Your servant and to his plea, O LORD my God, listening to the cry and to the prayer that Your servant prays before You this day, that Your eyes may be open night and day toward this house, the place of which You have said, "*My name shall be there,*" that You may listen to the prayer that Your servant offers toward this place. And listen to the plea of Your servant and of Your people Israel, when they pray toward this place. *And listen in heaven Your dwelling place, and when You hear, for-*

give. (1 Kings 8:27–30; emphasis added)

God's sacred covenant name (Yahweh) was holy, known, and one with His sacred presence for forgiveness. In the New Testament, Jesus Himself (the answer to Solomon's question, "Will God indeed dwell on earth?") tells us, "Go therefore and make disciples of all nations, baptizing them in the *name* of the Father and of the Son and of the Holy Spirit" (Matthew 28:19; emphasis added). The sacred and holy name of God is placed on me in Baptism. I am clothed with Christ ("For as many of you as were baptized into Christ have put on Christ" [Galatians 3:27]). Not only that, God in Christ dwells in me by His Spirit (Galatians 2:20). By virtue of Christ, I am regarded as holy, and by the working of His Spirit through the Word, I am continuously sanctified even as I struggle daily with sin. This is possible because God's name is holy in itself. It sanctifies what it touches. "This name should . . . be valued holy and grand as the greatest treasure and holy thing that we have" (LC III 38).

. . . but we pray in this petition that it may be kept holy among us also.

God's name in the Gospel of free forgiveness, creates what it requires, faith. God's name cannot be separated from or set at odds with His own clear and powerful Word. "If you abide in My word, you are truly My disciples, and you will know the truth, and the truth will set you free" (John 8:31–32). The Triune God, Father, Son, and Holy Spirit, who has claimed us, wants us to keep His name holy. We do this "when both our doctrine and life are godly and Christian" (LC III 39).

How is God's name kept holy? God's name is kept holy when the Word of God is taught in its truth and purity,

The Bible is a large book. It has been described as "a river so shallow a child can wade across, and so deep it can drown an elephant." But its basic teachings (the Ten Commandments, creation, redemption, sanctification, the Lord's Prayer, Baptism,

Confession and Absolution, and the Lord's Supper) are extremely clear and easy to understand if we but hold to the very words of the Bible itself. The Small Catechism exists for this very purpose. Jesus said, "Man does not live by bread alone, but by every word that comes from the mouth of God" (Matthew 4:4). It is not only possible to know the truth of what God teaches in the Bible, God requires that we believe it, hold to it, and see that it is taught rightly. When one dares to teach something as God's truth that is not true and contradicts the clear words of the Bible, it is a violation of the Second Commandment, an offense to His name. "We pray that His name not be taken in vain to swear, curse, lie, deceive, and so on, but be used well for God's praise and honor" (LC III 45). False teaching may also rob us and others of the Gospel itself! It's serious! That's why St. Paul wrote, "But even if we or an angel from heaven should preach to you a gospel contrary to the one we preached to you, let him be accursed" (Galatians 1:8).

. . . and we, as the children of God, also lead holy lives according to it. Help us to do this, dear Father in heaven!

God calls us not merely to believe aright; we are also to live aright. This means avoiding gross outward sins like "swearing, cursing, conjuring" (LC III 42), deceit, theft, drunkenness, sexual sins, greed, slander, and unkindness. It means, too, that when we fall into such outward sins, or even sins of thought, we are to repent quickly, confess our sins, and believe the Gospel for forgiveness.

The Large Catechism says, "To hallow means the same as to praise, magnify, and honor both in word and deed" (LC III 46). God's gifts and answered prayer give us unsurpassed joy. I have joy that I know exactly who God is. I know His name. I know I am forgiven in His Son. I know His name is mine in Holy Baptism. I know I am His beloved child. I know He expects me to sanctify His name in word and deed. I know He answers my prayer, "Hallowed by Thy name."

But anyone who teaches or lives contrary to God's Word profanes the name of God among us. Protect us from this, heavenly Father!

This is a prayer to pull me into the Holy Scriptures, that I may know the full truth of Christ, growing from milk to solid food. This is a prayer that I study the Small and Large Catechisms that I may know by heart the chief teachings of the Gospel. This is a prayer that I be a vigilant (though kind) member of my church, always insisting on God's Word and nothing but. "But we have renounced disgraceful, underhanded ways. We refuse to practice cunning or to tamper with God's word, but by the open statement of the truth we would commend ourselves to everyone's conscience in the sight of God" (2 Corinthians 4:2).

Why am I Joy:fully Lutheran?

I am Joy:fully Lutheran because I know the name of the One to whom I pray, and I know clearly what it is to hallow His name. He wills that I pray that—by His grace—I hallow His name as much as I can; that I see that His Word "is taught in its truth and purity"; and that I believe and live accordingly. It's clear.

O Father, Son, and Holy Spirit, You **instruct** me that Your name is holy. You dwelt with Your name and presence in the temple for forgiveness. You dwell in Christ bodily for forgiveness (John 1:14). You dwell in Baptism in Your blessed name to forgive me and place Your name on me for eternal blessings.

I **thank** You, O almighty and triune God, that You have revealed Your name and Your blessed Gospel and Sacraments in the Holy Scriptures, causing them all to be written for my faith and salvation, and that You have called me by Your name to honor You in word and deed.

I **confess**, my God, that I have so often failed to sanctify Your name. I've been sluggish at reading the Bible. I don't know Your Word as I ought. I am captivated and led astray at times by worldly wisdom and, sadly, not only in thought and word but in sinful action.

O Jesus! O Father! O Spirit! Your name be hallowed! For the sake of Your redeeming name, forgive me! Cause me to hallow Your name, love Your Word, and live accordingly and joyously as Your own! Amen.

CHAPTER 17

THE SECOND PETITION
Thy kingdom come.

> *What does this mean?* The kingdom* of God certainly comes by itself without our prayer, but we pray in this petition that it may come to us also.

> *How does God's kingdom come?* God's kingdom comes when our heavenly Father gives us His Holy Spirit, so that by His grace we believe His holy Word and lead godly lives here in time and there in eternity.

For the kingdom of God is not a matter of eating and drinking but of righteousness and peace and joy in the Holy Spirit. **(ROMANS 14:17)**

What does this mean? The kingdom of God certainly comes by itself without our prayer,

Thanks be to God. This is a wonderful, mysterious, and joyous truth. The kingdom of God depends on Him, not us. In the First Petition, we pray, "Hallowed be Thy name." There we confess that "God's name is certainly holy in itself, but we pray in this petition that it may be kept holy among us also." God's name is holy. He delights in children who recognize that fact. God is the actor. The Holy Spirit is given "to bring . . . home to us" (LC III 51) all that Jesus has done for us, noted in the Second Article of the Creed. He does this by the Word. What Jesus said to and of His apostles is also true of all Christians. "You did not choose Me, but I chose you" (John 15:16).

This is the missionary petition of the Lord's Prayer. In the Large Catechism, Luther emphasizes two aspects: prayer for the Kingdom is prayer for ourselves, that we remain and grow in the Kingdom (a present reality for those who believe in Jesus), and prayer for others, that others throughout the world come into the Kingdom as well.

We pray that His name may be so praised through God's holy Word and a Christian life that we who have accepted it may abide and daily grow in it, and that it may gain approval and acceptance among other people. We pray that it may go forth with power throughout the world. (LC III 52)

On the one hand, God can and will save His elect with or without us. He brings about salvation, not us. On the other hand, it is His good pleasure to have His eternal Gospel spread by us Christians so that all may hear and believe. God is at work and shall be at work expanding His kingdom according to His will, quite despite us if necessary.

***How does God's kingdom come?* God's kingdom comes when our heavenly Father gives us His Holy Spirit, so that by His grace we believe His holy Word and lead godly lives here in time and there in eternity.**

The New Testament repeatedly defines coming to faith in Christ (i.e., coming into the Kingdom or Church) as a divinely worked resurrection. The Bible could not be clearer on this point.

And you were dead in the trespasses and sins in which you once walked, following the course of this world, following the prince of the power of the air, the spirit that is now at work in the sons of disobedience—among whom we all once lived in the passions of our flesh, carrying out the desires of the body and the mind, and were by nature children of wrath, like the rest of mankind. But God, being rich in mercy, because of the great love with which He loved us, even when we were dead in our trespasses, made us alive together with Christ—by grace you have been saved—and raised us up with Him and seated us with Him in the heavenly places in Christ Jesus, so that in the coming ages He might show the immeasurable riches of His grace in kindness toward us in

Christ Jesus. For by grace you have been saved through faith. And this is not your own doing; it is the gift of God, not a result of works, so that no one may boast. For we are His workmanship, created in Christ Jesus for good works, which God prepared beforehand, that we should walk in them. (Ephesians 2:1–10)

Note St. Paul's penetrating denial of human ability or free will regarding things spiritual.

The natural person does not accept the things of the Spirit of God, for they are folly to him, and he is not able to understand them because they are spiritually discerned. (1 Corinthians 2:14)

Think of it like Lazarus in the tomb. Jesus did not say, "Lazarus! I've done everything I could for you. Now it's up to you. It's your decision. What will it be?" That's ridiculous. But what did Jesus say? "Lazarus! Come out!" Then John's Gospel records, "The man who had died came out [of the tomb]" (John 11:43). The power to raise a dead man was in the Word of Jesus. That powerful Word continues to raise "the dead." Dead men don't "decide for Jesus."

When we state with the catechism, "The kingdom of God certainly comes by itself," we are acknowledging God is the actor. John the Baptizer (Matthew 3:2) and, soon after, Jesus Himself suddenly appeared, preaching, "Repent, for the kingdom of heaven is at hand" (Matthew 4:17). They preached Law (repent!) and Gospel (forgiveness of sins). By the power of the Spirit, working through the Word, many believed (all gift!).

This is very comforting. It points me to Jesus and His Word, not to myself. When I consider my deepest thoughts, my sinful desires, my failings, I despair. If I'm dishonest, I parade before God and people, denying and lying about my sins, making excuses, or worse, alleging I've got no real sins at all. When I look inside myself, I conjure ways to prepare myself for God's kingdom. I resolve to work harder. I convince my psyche to suppress the sinful truth about myself—I'm good enough for heaven! I'm certainly more prepared for the Kingdom than *that* person! Luther stated the plain truth in a penetrating way in his book *On the Bondage of the Will.*

> The Kingdom is not to be prepared, but is already prepared. The children of the Kingdom are prepared rather than them preparing the Kingdom. This means: The Kingdom earns the children, not the children the Kingdom. (Peters, *Lord's Prayer*, 75; see also AE 33:153)

God grants faith by the Holy Spirit. We believe His Holy Word, and in His kingdom we "lead godly lives here in time and there in eternity." He wills to use even us for His evangelistic purposes. "You are a chosen race, a royal priesthood, a holy nation, a people for His own possession, that you may proclaim the excellencies of Him who called you out of darkness into His marvelous light" (1 Peter 2:9). Our joyous privilege is to speak of Christ to those who do not know Him (most often people right under our noses, in our very houses and families!), as the woman at the well did. "'Come, see a man who told me all that I ever did. Can this be the Christ?' They went out of the town and were coming to Him" (John 4:29–30). "Many Samaritans from that town believed in Him because of the woman's testimony" (John 4:39). How marvelous that Jesus uses sinners and unlikely saints to bring others into the Kingdom!

One more note. The "kingdom of God" is the Church. It comes in two ways: in time and in eternity (LC III 53). According to Jesus, it is a present reality wherever one encounters and believes Jesus in the Word of God (Church Militant). "For behold, the kingdom of God is in the midst of you" (Luke 17:21). And the Kingdom as the Church Triumphant stretches into eternity, where the saints await its joyous consummation at the end of time. "Truly, I say to you, I will not drink again of the fruit of the vine until that day when I drink it new in the kingdom of God" (Mark 14:25).

This petition of the Lord's Prayer teaches us that in leading godly lives the beginning, middle, and end of all of the Church's mission is prayer: Thy kingdom come.

WHY AM I JOY:FULLY LUTHERAN?

I am Joy:fully Lutheran because God's kingdom comes of itself and by His action. He has not only brought me to His kingdom, but He also wills to use even me in bringing His kingdom to others. And His kingdom is joy.

Dear Lord Christ, in this petition, You **instruct** us to humbly pray for ourselves and for all people, and we and all people may come into Your kingdom by faith in Your blessed cross and resurrection.

O Lord, I give **thanks** that Your kingdom comes of itself and is not thwarted by my lack of prayer and failure to confess Your name. I give You even greater thanks that You have determined to spread Your kingdom through fallible people like me.

I **confess**, O Lord, my lack of zeal in prayer, my lack of confidence in Your Word and promises, and my fear of sharing Your name where You have placed me.

O Jesus, Thy kingdom come! Forgive me my many sins! Let Your kingdom continue to come to me! Let Your kingdom come in my family, in my community, in my congregation. I pray You, Lord, "send out laborers into the harvest" (Matthew 9:38). Use me, Lord, as You see fit! Loosen my lips to pray. Open my mouth to tell. Open my ears to hear Your Word. Open my heart to love those around me who need You. Amen.

THE THIRD PETITION
Thy will be done on earth as it is in heaven.

What does this mean? The good and gracious will of God is done even without our prayer, but we pray in this petition that it may be done among us also.

How is God's will done? God's will is done

when He breaks and hinders every evil plan and purpose of the devil, the world, and our sinful nature, which do not want us to hallow God's name or let His kingdom come;

and when He strengthens and keeps us firm in His Word and faith until we die.

This is His good and gracious will.

And He said, "Abba, Father, all things are possible for You. Remove this cup from Me. Yet not what I will, but what You will." **(MARK 14:36)**

What does this mean? **The good and gracious will of God is done even without our prayer,**

The Small Catechism continues the pattern of explaining and expanding on the previous petitions. God's name will be hallowed. God's kingdom will come. God's will will be done. In the Lord's Prayer, we acknowledge that this is true, and we especially pray that these all may be done in our lives.

As we have said before, we pray that what must be done without us anyway may also be done in us. As His name must be hallowed and His kingdom come whether we pray or not, so also His will must be done and succeed. (LC III 68)

. . . but we pray in this petition that it may be done among us also.

There is a twofold Law/Gospel aspect to the will of God "done among us also." Thus Jesus preached, "Not everyone who says to Me, 'Lord, Lord,' will enter the kingdom of heaven, but the one who does the will of My Father who is in heaven" (Matthew 7:21). This is, of course, Law. Jesus follows this with the threat of hell to those who claim faith in Him, yet intentionally act contrary to the will of God. Of course, through the centuries, all those in the Church who have joylessly thought salvation is earned in whole or in part by following the Law understood "the will of God" in such terms. The Law is certainly true, and Jesus' preaching of it is truer still. But its purpose is not to get us to heaven. "The Law is but a mirror bright To bring the in-bred sin to light" (*LSB* 555:3). The Law is given "so that every mouth may be stopped, and . . . held accountable to God" (Romans 3:19). The will of God as Law to be obeyed, and therefore as Law to bring repentance, moves toward the ultimate will of God that by faith we hallow God's name (faith in Christ) and that His kingdom come to us.

Thus God's will is that we believe the joyous Gospel of forgiveness in Christ, hold fast to Christ in time—come what may—and spend eternity with Him and all the saints in His heavenly kingdom. God is the actor who achieves His will, which He "does among us also."

How is God's will done?

We don't pray here so much that we do the will of God, but rather that He accomplish His will in our lives and deeds and especially by giving us faith that endures every assault until we rejoice with Him in eternity.

God's will is done when He breaks and hinders every evil plan and purpose of the devil,

Satan is a liar and the father of lies. "You are of your father the devil, and your will is to do your father's desires. He was a murderer from the beginning, and does not stand in the truth, because there is no truth in him. When he lies, he speaks out of his own character, for he is a liar and the father of lies" (John 8:44). Satan tempted Jesus when He was weak after forty days of fasting. To each temptation, Jesus responded, "It is written." The devil tempted Jesus arrogantly to test God the Father's care, and he did so quoting the Bible himself! "If You are the Son of God, throw Yourself down, for it is written . . . 'On their hands they will bear you up, lest you strike your foot against a stone'" (Matthew 4:5–6). Jesus responded, "Again it is written, 'You shall not put the Lord your God to the test'" (v. 7). Finally, Satan tempted Jesus by showing Him "all the kingdoms of the world" (v. 8). Again Jesus responded, "Be gone, Satan! For it is written, 'You shall worship the Lord your God and Him only shall you serve'" (v. 10).

What do we learn? First and most important, Jesus accomplished the will of God, against Satan, for us, and in our place. As in the case of the temptation of Christ, Satan strikes at our weakest moments at our most vulnerable points. The best defense against the temptations of the devil is faith in Jesus, who overcame the devil, the world, and the flesh by His great death and resurrection, and familiarity with the Bible as God's own powerful words (including what the Bible gives us with respect to Baptism, Absolution, and the Lord's Supper). The devil himself knows the Bible and will twist its words to encourage us to sin. This fact bids us know the Scriptures' basic teachings (the Six Chief Parts of the Catechism!), to read and study the Bible daily, and to regard preaching and His Word as "sacred and gladly hear and learn it" (Small Catechism, Third Commandment). This is God's will for us.

The worst onslaught of the devil is to trouble our consciences about our sins and thereby lead us to commit the worst of all sins: to doubt the all-sufficient sacrifice of Christ for all our sins of thought, word, and deed. Doubt that the blood of God in the flesh is sufficient payment for my pusillanimous, paltry, and pathetic run-of-the-mill sins is the ultimate blasphemy. Satan will continue to harass us, but he's been thrown down. The devil's plan and will has been broken by Christ. He cannot win the day.

> And I heard a loud voice in heaven, saying, "Now the salvation and the power and the kingdom of our God and the authority of His Christ have come, for the accuser of our brothers has been thrown down, who accuses them day and night before our God." (Revelation 12:10)

. . . the world,

It is the will of God that we recognize the wondrous bounty and beauty of creation as God's own doing and gift to us to be treasured and used appropriately (First Article!). But *world* is a code word in the New Testament for creatures distorted by sin and moved by lust, evil desire, selfishness, impurity, and greed, with a continual lust for more (see Ephesians 4:17–19). The world is the devil's tool. "He provokes the world against us, fans and stirs the fire, so that he may hinder and drive us back, cause us to fall, and again bring us under his power" (LC III 63).

. . . and our sinful nature,

Luther used the words "our flesh." Jesus said, "The flesh is no help at all" (John 6:63). It is the continual corruption and impulse to sin found in every one of us. In Christ, we have victory over sin, death, the devil, and our flesh. But we continue to struggle daily with this impulse to sin. Being a Christian is not a matter of becoming sinless. That won't happen in this life. Anyone who claims to have achieved such perfection is a fool and a liar. A Christian knows Jesus covers his or her sin, and yet is in the struggle against the "old Adam" every day of life. St. Paul describes the struggle in Romans 7.

> For I know that nothing good dwells in me, that is, in my flesh. For I have the desire to do what is right, but not the ability to carry it out. For I do not do the good I want, but the evil I do not want is what I keep on doing. Now if I do what I do not want, it is no longer I who do it, but sin that dwells within me.

So I find it to be a law that when I want to do right, evil lies close at hand. For I delight in the law of God, in my inner being, but I see in my members another law waging war against the law of my mind and making me captive to the law of sin that dwells in my members. Wretched man that I am! Who will deliver me from this body of death? Thanks be to God through Jesus Christ our Lord! So then, I myself serve the law of God with my mind, but with my flesh I serve the law of sin. (Romans 7:18–25)

. . . which do not want us to hallow God's name or let His kingdom come;

The devil, the world, and our flesh all set before us the prospect of joy. But it is pseudojoy, which takes us away from God's name and kingdom. The promise is gratification of desire for wealth, sex, honor, statues, you name it. But its joy is a mirage. Again, it was Augustine who said, "Our hearts are restless till they find rest in Thee" (*Confessions* 1.1.4; *NPNF* 1/1:45).

. . . and when He strengthens and keeps us firm in His Word and faith until we die.

The path to joy is a surprising one. It's the way of the cross. He strengthens us in a strange way: through suffering. Jesus Himself prayed this petition in the garden, on the way to the cross.

And going a little farther He fell on His face and prayed, saying, "My Father, if it be possible, let this cup pass from Me; nevertheless, not as I will, but as You will." . . . Again, for the second time, He went away and prayed, "My Father, if this cannot pass unless I drink it, Your will be done." (Matthew 26:39, 42)

This incident provides a profound answer to a challenging and often troubling question. Does God will suffering? In Jesus, we see that the answer is yes. There were many guilty players in the crucifixion of Christ. But finally, it was the will of God that He sent His Son to suffer. And it was Jesus' own will to suffer and die for all (John 10:18). In Jesus, we see that suffering is purposeful and is the path to resurrection and joy.

So also in the lives of Christians. We don't know exactly what it was, but Paul was given (by God Himself!) a thorn.

> So to keep me from becoming conceited because of the surpassing greatness of the revelations, a thorn was given me in the flesh, a messenger of Satan to harass me, to keep me from becoming conceited. Three times I pleaded with the Lord about this, that it should leave me. But He said to me, "My grace is sufficient for you, for My power is made perfect in weakness." Therefore I will boast all the more gladly of my weaknesses, so that the power of Christ may rest upon me. For the sake of Christ, then, I am content with weaknesses, insults, hardships, persecutions, and calamities. For when I am weak, then I am strong. (2 Corinthians 12:7–10)

While God is not the cause or author of sin, we can see from St. Paul that it was God's will that a messenger of Satan harass him. Luther says in the Large Catechism that the devil, the world, and the flesh advance against us, and "we shall have to suffer many thrusts and blows" (LC III 61).

WHY AM I JOY:FULLY LUTHERAN?

Because the devil, the world, and even the flesh ("a thorn was given me in the flesh") are God's monkeys. He sets their limit. Their time is short. They are on a chain. And at the joyous last, we shall rejoice to say to them what Joseph said to his brothers, "You meant evil against me, but God meant it for good" (Genesis 50:20). Suffering, even suffering my weaknesses of the flesh, drives me to Jesus. And that is God's good and gracious will. So we pray with Jesus, "Let this cup pass from us. But not our will, but Yours be done." **This is His good and gracious will.**

Almighty and everlasting God, Father, Son, and Holy Spirit, by Your Word You **instruct** me that it is Your will that Your name be hallowed, that Your kingdom come. I pray that Your will be done everywhere, and especially in me. It is Your will that I believe the Gospel and have eternal life.

I **thank** You, my God, that I know Your will clearly from Your Holy Scriptures. I thank You, too, that I know from the Scriptures and from the cross itself that You mysteriously will suffering for my good.

I **confess**, dear Lord, that all too often I consent to the will of the devil, the world, and my sinful flesh, seeking joy where it will not be and never has been found. For true joy is found in Jesus.

Dear Lord, guard me against the assaults of the devil, the world, and the flesh. When I suffer weaknesses, drive me to You. Use the suffering in my life just as You used thorns in the life of St. Paul. When I find myself in the garden with Jesus, help me to pray, "Thy will be done on earth as it is in heaven." Amen.

CHAPTER 19

THE FOURTH PETITION
Give us this day our daily bread.

> *What does this mean?* God certainly gives daily bread to everyone without our prayers, even to all evil people, but we pray in this petition that God would lead us to realize this and to receive our daily bread with thanksgiving.

> *What is meant by daily bread?* Daily bread includes everything that has to do with the support and needs of the body, such as food, drink, clothing, shoes, house, home, land, animals, money, goods, a devout husband or wife, devout children, devout workers, devout and faithful rulers, good government, good weather, peace, health, self-control, good reputation, good friends, faithful neighbors, and the like.

There is nothing better for a person than that
he should eat and drink and find enjoyment in
his toil. This also, I saw, is from the hand of God.
(ECCLESIASTES 2:24)

Wow. "Give us this day our daily bread." Seven simple words. One short phrase. I pray it daily, often several times. I pray it in church. As it rolls over my lips, if I'm lucky, I think in a flash of a loaf of bread before scurrying on to the rest of the Lord's Prayer, the next part of the Sunday liturgy, a psalm, prayers for specific needs, people, and the like.

The Small Catechism's explanations of the three "Thy" petitions that precede this one emphasize the objectivity of God's gifts. Likewise, the catechism emphasizes in this first "us" petition that daily bread comes "to everyone without our prayers." The joyously transformative moments of life occur when we suddenly realize that "daily bread" encompasses a very broad panoply of blessings (the whole First Article!) and that these blessings are showered, even unloaded, on us with such frequency, such intensity, and such immensity that when we become aware of them, we are overwhelmed and transformed with humble, thankful joy.

. . . but we pray in this petition that God would lead us to realize this and to receive our daily bread with thanksgiving.

Here's the point. The objective fact of Christ's life, death, and resurrection stands. "In Christ God was reconciling the world to Himself" (2 Corinthians 5:19). Jesus "was delivered up for our trespasses and raised for our justification" (Romans 4:25). The sin—all sin—of the world has been paid for. The benefit of Christ's act is obtained solely by the gracious gift of faith. Faith lays hold of Christ and all His benefits. "Not having a righteousness of my own that comes from the law, but that which comes through faith in Christ, the righteousness from God that depends on faith" (Philippians 3:9). God's name is holy. Dear Lord, grant that I hallow it! God's kingdom comes. Dear Lord, grant that it comes and remains with me! God's will be done. Dear Lord, grant that Your will be done in me and that I recognize it as such! So also, when I pray, "Give us this day our daily bread," I pray, "Lord, open my blind eyes to see the abundant shower of Your blessings!"

To receive our daily bread with thanksgiving is a matter of faith in God, Father, Son, and Holy Spirit. One may be cognizant of all the gifts in creation (First Article), but without faith in the Son of God and explicit knowledge of all that has been done (Second Article) and continues to be done by the Holy Spirit to grant faith and gather the Church (Third Article), I would be ignorant of the Trinity to whom my thankfulness is directed. Like St. Paul himself, "I know whom I have believed, and I am convinced that He is able to guard until that day what has been entrusted to me" (2 Timothy 1:12).

It is God's express will that Christians rejoice and give

thanks. "Rejoice always, pray without ceasing, give thanks in all circumstances; for this is the will of God in Christ Jesus for you" (1 Thessalonians 5:16–18). Such rejoicing is not so much a command as a gracious gift. In fact, the words in the New Testament for *rejoice* and *grace* come from the same root. Rejoicing results from faith's recognition of the plethora of God's gifts, whether of salvation (Second and Third Articles) or creation (First Article). "Only and exclusively in the redemption through Christ, the fatherly goodness of the Creator is revealed in final clarity" (Peters, *Lord's Prayer*, 140). So it's no happenstance that we pray first in the Lord's Prayer for faith, God's kingdom, and His will for us before we pray for daily bread.

By the third and fourth centuries of the Church's life, the interpretation of "daily bread" moved toward the Lord's Supper. In fact, it became the central theme through the Middle Ages. This is in part because the word for *daily* used in the Gospels can also be translated "supersubstantial" or "supernatural." And of course, there are wonderful and comforting references to Jesus as the bread of heaven to be eaten in John 6. "Bread" in the sense of daily needs was never lost in the Church's interpretation through the centuries. While Luther did not reject outright a sacramental interpretation of "daily bread," he did anchor the Fourth Petition in creation. "He richly and daily provides me with all that I need to support this body and life" (Apostles' Creed, First Article). And the list of created blessings in the explanation of the First Article very closely mirrors the list in the explanation of this petition.

The story of Zacchaeus strikes me as precisely a Fourth Petition miracle. And with all the grousing negativity of the devil, the world, and my flesh, the miracle of Jesus is what I need most to have my eyes opened to my God's fatherly hand of blessing.

> And when Jesus came to the place, He looked up and said to him, "Zacchaeus, hurry and come down, for I must stay at your house today." So he hurried and came down and received Him joyfully. And when they saw it,

they all grumbled, "He has gone in to be the guest of a man who is a sinner." And Zacchaeus stood and said to the Lord, "Behold, Lord, the half of my goods I give to the poor. And if I have defrauded anyone of anything, I restore it fourfold." And Jesus said to him, "Today salvation has come to this house, since he also is a son of Abraham. For the Son of Man came to seek and to save the lost." (Luke 19:5–10)

What a profound event. The words and deeds of Jesus caused faith in Zacchaeus. He was known as a sinner—especially for greed and misuse of his and others' First Article possessions—and an abuser of his office as tax collector. Jesus changes everything. As with Zacchaeus, faith in Christ brings us joy. It welcomes Him also into our homes—the economic capital of our existence on this earth. My death grip on money and possessions is loosened. The rigor mortis of self-centeredness become a living generosity. Suddenly I realize my wealth is all gift and God keeps it coming. With Luther, I look at my hand and see that "God has made holes between the fingers so that money falls out easily." The Christian rights economic wrongs and restores possessions. And the joyous and thankful Christian restores offices of service and relationships. What a transformation.

What is meant by daily bread? Daily bread includes everything that has to do with the support and needs of the body, such as food, drink,

"Go, eat your bread with joy, and drink your wine with a merry heart, for God has already approved what you do" (Ecclesiastes 9:7). Transform me, O Lord. Open my eyes to see You and Your blessings in all food and drink that You provide me and all people. You provide me the "living bread" in Your Sacrament (John 6:51), a foretaste of the coming heavenly feast! You have sustained me from my mother's arms to this very moment. What an amazing array of delicacies You have set before me all these years. Give me moderation in food and drink, even as I recognize Your blessings and Christian freedom in their use (Romans 14). Grant food and drink to the hungry! I rejoice in and thank You for Your blessings!

. . . clothing, shoes,

"Grant to those who mourn in Zion—to give them a beautiful headdress instead of ashes, the oil of gladness instead of mourning, the garment of praise instead of a faint spirit; that they may be called oaks of righteousness, the planting of the LORD, that He may be glorified" (Isaiah 61:3). Every day of my thankless life, dear God, You have provided me clothing and shoes. I've been protected and cared for with diapers, a baptismal garment, playclothes, Sunday best, clothes in which I learned the value of hard work, clothes for fun with family and friends, clothes for marriage, clothes for my children, clothes for saying goodbye to loved ones, and clothes for joyous occasions. Yet I think nothing of it. Forgive me, O Lord. Protect those in challenging places who make clothing. Care for "the sojourner, giving him food and clothing" (Deuteronomy 10:18). Bring and keep them in faith in Christ! Cause every sock, every pant leg, every suit, every T-shirt to be for me a cause of thanksgiving and generosity!

. . . house, home,

Dear Jesus, make me Your Zacchaeus. Say to me, "Hurry and come down, for I must stay at your house today" (Luke 19:5). How gracious You have been to me throughout my pathetic and thankless life. You have provided a house for my protection and that of my family. Wherever I have gone, whatever vocations I've enjoyed, You have placed a roof over my head. And You have made my houses homes. You've filled them with Christians. You have graced them with dear friends. You have sent people in need. You have sent those who do not know You to hear Your Gospel. You have sent babies, children, and young men. You have sent elderly parents. You have given communities of love and care. Turn my stingy heart. Forgive the sins committed in my home. Make me Your joyous Zacchaeus. Make me generous. Give me the strength to right wrongs. Come dwell in my house and make it a home.

. . . land, animals,

Dear Jesus, Your gifts abound. I come from families of farmers. Generations worked the land, tended animals, created a storehouse of wealth. You were behind the sweat of the brow. You are the giver. You are Giver and Creator of every new life, calf or human baby. You, through Your Word and the gifts of honest labor, created a people thankful to be Your children by faith. You continue to bless us all with the gifts of agriculture for food and clothing, fuel, and products too numerous to mention. How often I behold Your bounty as I travel the country and the world, yet I think little of it. Forgive my small mind and heart. I rejoice in Your blessings and give thanks. Remind me daily that a joyful and thankful heart shares the bounty of blessings.

. . . money, goods,

O gracious God, Your beloved Son said, "It is easier for a camel to go through the eye of a needle than for a rich man to enter the kingdom of God" (Luke 18:25). I am a rich man. Even the poorest of the poor in the United States is wealthy by world standards. Money and possessions are gifts. They are not evil. Your apostle said, "The *love* of money is a root of all kinds of evils" (1 Timothy 6:10; emphasis added). The Bible condemns greed (Matthew 23:25), but also praises the blessings of hard work and wealth (2 Timothy 2:6). O God, smash the strongbox I've made in my heart for money and goods. Destroy my idol of greed. Be my God alone. Render all I have a servant of good. Make me joyful. Make me thankful. Render me a blessing to my church, my pastor, and those in need of Your love.

. . . a devout husband or wife,

Beloved Savior, You have blessed me with a wife. She is a Christian. She is a complement to our household, to our vocational lives, to our children. She is loyal. Forgive my failures to care for her, to lead her into prayer, to serve her with Your own love (Ephesians 5). Forgive me for taking her and the blessings that encompass her for granted. I repent. Restore my joy. Thank You for her gracious heart. Through cross and trial, through every joy and sorrow shared, make me the spouse You would have me be. Let Your Word work its power in me, in my wife, and in all spouses and all homes. Let me be joyous and thankful to You for her. "Let your fountain be blessed, and rejoice in the wife of your youth" (Proverbs 5:18).

. . . devout children,

Ever gracious Father, model of fatherhood, when I survey the mistakes I have made with my children, the moments of anger and frustration, the time I've spent occupied with work, I marvel at Your grace. My children love me still. This is all gift. They love You, O Lord, and in Your fatherly care, in the blessed name of Your Son, they love even me. They forgive each other. They forgive their parents. And they rejoice and give thanks to You. "Let Israel be glad in his Maker; let the children of Zion rejoice in their King!" (Psalm 149:2).

. . . devout workers,

Kind Creator of all vocations, You set Adam about working the garden. Sin made work difficult. Christ redeems all vocations. As I and others work to serve others, render us humble. For Your Son serves me. "The Son of Man came not to be served but to serve, and to give His life as a ransom for many" (Matthew 20:28). Grant me faith to be fair, charitable, and kind to all who labor, to encourage them, to be thankful for them and to them, never failing to note that every honorable vocation, no matter how humble or despised by the world, is God's own gift. Such laborers are the hands of God.

. . . devout and faithful rulers,

Mighty God, You remove and establish the rulers of this

earth. You "bring princes to nothing, and make the rulers of the earth as emptiness" (Isaiah 40:23). All rulers, kings, queens, presidents, prime ministers, and princes, whether they know it or not, exercise authority bestowed by You. Thwart tyrants. Open minds and hearts to allow the proclamation of the Gospel and the free course of religion. For such rulers have no power over the conscience. How often I have bemoaned our leaders over the decades. How paltry have been my prayers for them. How uncharitable my judgments. Even the worst of leaders—so far as they keep order and allow the Gospel—are a blessing to me and all people (Romans 13). Forgive us our joyless thanklessness for the blessings we do enjoy, and grant us good leaders. "I urge that . . . prayers . . . and thanksgivings be made for all people, for kings and all who are in high positions, that we may lead a peaceful and quiet life, godly and dignified in every way" (1 Timothy 2:1–2).

. . . good government,

Most Holy Trinity, You have taught us in your clear Word that good government is established by You, punishes evil, maintains good order, protects its citizens, remedies injustice, protects the innocent, collects taxes for good purposes (Romans 13:1–7), and does not attempt to control thoughts or peaceful religious practice (see Acts 5:29). Thwart bad government, especially where it is allowing the killing of the unborn and aged, acting unjustly or allowing unjust action, failing to protect its citizens, undermining marriage and family, and not allowing the Gospel free course. I thank You, Lord, for the many faithful Christians and honest non-Christians in governments around the world, who uphold just law. May their number increase and due honor be given them. "Pay to all what is owed to them: taxes to whom taxes are owed, revenue to whom revenue is owed, respect to whom respect is owed, honor to whom honor is owed" (Romans 13:7).

. . . good weather,

Gracious Savior, how little I have contemplated the blessed change of seasons, the sending of rain at opportune times. How little do I understand the marvelous complexity of the world You have created. How often have I doubted Your benevolence in the face of overwhelming hurricanes, flood, fire, and disaster. In the wake of disaster, grant repentance and faith. In times of great natural tragedy, I plunge my thoughts into the depths of Your wounds on the cross, there trusting that "all things work together for good, for those who are called according to . . . [Your] purpose" (Romans 8:28). Give us joy in sharing with and caring for those struck by disaster. Give us joy and thankfulness for good weather.

. . . peace,

Prince of Peace, Mighty God, Wonderful Counselor, thwart the will of the devil, the world, and our sinful flesh. Thwart the continual lust for power and territory. Thwart all who would use religion as a pretense for unjust and illegal expansion of kingdoms. Cause the community of nations to act with prudence but decisively against rulers and nations bent on unjust purposes. In horrendous times of the necessity of defensive war, grant quick and decisive victory to the just. When corrupt powers collide, use "one knave [to punish] . . . another" (LC I 154). Forgive me my failure to use times of peace to spread the Gospel. Forgive my thankless heart. Help me to honor those who serve the nation justly. And use every conflict to cause us to look to Jesus, who "is our peace" (Ephesians 2:14), and to an eternal kingdom. "Of the increase of His government and of peace there will be no end" (Isaiah 9:7).

. . . health,

Great Physician, in Your earthly walk You healed the sick and even raised the dead. Forgive my poor stewardship of the body You have given me. I humbly admit that I fail constantly to thank You for the good health with which You have blessed me.

I pray with faint fervor when I'm facing illness or the illness of a loved one, but I pray even less in thanksgiving for Your constant blessings and just a little for the healing I observe. I know it is Your pleasure when I enjoy good health. I also know You invite me to pray for my health and that of others. Forgive me, Lord. Sustain all those who are suffering. According to Your will, remove the illness and restore to health. Cause all honorable medical professions to flourish, and bless those who exercise these vocations. If it be Your will that I should suffer, cause me to recognize even under the "messenger of Satan" (2 Corinthians 12:7) Your all-powerful hand and hidden purpose, just as St. Paul did. "My grace is sufficient for you, for My power is made perfect in weakness" (2 Corinthians 12:9). Cause me, wretch that I am, to see God's hand at work at all times and, like Paul, to "rejoice in . . . [my] sufferings" (Romans 5:3).

. . . self-control,

Jesus, God in the flesh and Lord of all humility, modesty, and self-control, You refused the traps of Satan to exercise Your authority for sinful purpose and temporal gain (Matthew 4). How often I have lacked discipline. How often my words have hurt another, even threatening his or her livelihood. How a lack of self-control destroys home after home, pits spouses against each other, destroys families, children, and relationships. Lack of discipline is at the heart of sins of lust, fornication, greed, theft, drunkenness, and covetousness. All of these make our temporal lives miserable and destroy eternal life by snuffing out faith. Grow in me the fruit of the Spirit, especially the last. "But the fruit of the Spirit is love, joy, peace, patience, kindness, goodness, faithfulness, gentleness, self-control; against such things there is no law" (Galatians 5:22–23).

. . . good reputation,

Eternal Word Incarnate, blessed Jesus, by You—the Word—heaven and earth were created. By a word, You have declared me righteous. Your powerful Word puts to death and makes alive.

"See now that I, even I, am He, and there is no god beside Me; I kill and I make alive; I wound and I heal; and there is none that can deliver out of My hand" (Deuteronomy 32:39). There is no power like Your Word, yet my words can work terrible damage. "So also the tongue is a small member, yet it boasts of great things. How great a forest is set ablaze by such a small fire!" (James 3:5). Damage to reputation can harm terribly one's temporal well-being. Lord, forgive my gossip and slander. Help me to go directly to the one with whom I have trouble (Matthew 18). Help me to let my ears be a tomb when I hear evil things spoken of others. Guard my tongue. I thank You for a good reputation. I rejoice where I am slandered because I follow You (Matthew 5:11–12). When I hear evil of my neighbor, help me to "defend him, speak well of him, and explain everything in the kindest way" (explanation of the Eighth Commandment).

. . . good friends, faithful neighbors, and the like.

Dearest Jesus was "a friend of tax collectors and sinners," much to the chagrin of the Pharisees (Matthew 11:19). Jesus regarded Lazarus as "our friend" (John 11:11) There are few pleasures more profound and joyous than friends who know you and love you still. There are few experiences more painful than the loss of a dear friend or neighbor. I must confess, Lord, that I have taken my friends for granted. I have often failed to encourage them and especially to pray for them. You have given neighbors throughout my life who are trustworthy and look after my well-being. Forgive my thanklessness. I rejoice in Your blessings! Help me to find ever greater joy in my friends. "Oil and perfume make the heart glad, and the sweetness of a friend comes from his earnest counsel" (Proverbs 27:9). And help me, Lord, to be such a friend and neighbor. "A friend loves at all times, and a brother is born for adversity" (Proverbs 17:17).

Why am I Joy:fully Lutheran?

I know my God, Father, Son, and Holy Spirit. The triune God has removed the scales from my eyes to see the fullness of His unending grace in Jesus and the bounty of His gifts to support this body and life. I am free. I am free from the punishment my sins deserve. And I am free to be generous to others.

Lord God, You **instruct** me in this petition to pray confidently, "Give us this day our daily bread." And by this, You mean that we are to pray daily for all that supports this body and life.

I **thank** You, Lord, that, before I ever prayed and before I pray even today, You have showered and continue to shower Your blessings on me and all people. I thank You also for hearing my humble prayers and answering them.

I **confess** that amid the overwhelming abundance of Your blessings I am coldhearted when it comes to prayer. I rarely recall the plenitude of Your mercy. I take for granted daily blessings that abound.

O God, forgive me. Renew me. Open my eyes to see Your unending love and care for me and all people. By Your Gospel, move my cold heart to pray. Cause me to look on all these creaturely blessings with joy and thankfulness. Amen.

CHAPTER 20

The Fifth Petition
And forgive us our trespasses as we forgive those who trespass against us.

> *What does this mean?* We pray in this petition that our Father in heaven would not look at our sins, or deny our prayer because of them. We are neither worthy of the things for which we pray, nor have we deserved them, but we ask that He would give them all to us by grace, for we daily sin much and surely deserve nothing but punishment. So we too will sincerely forgive and gladly do good to those who sin against us.

Restore to me the joy of Your salvation.
(PSALM 51:12)

This petition cuts like a razor of divine salvific action into our messy, sin-distorted, prodigal lives. As Luther says in the Large Catechism:

> Although we have and believe God's Word, do and submit to His will, and are supported by His gifts and blessings, our life is still not sinless. We still stumble daily and transgress because we live in the world among people. They do us much harm and give us reasons for impatience, anger, revenge, and such. (LC III 86)

Wonder of wonders, God bids us pray for what we need most, and what we deserve least, in the confident imperative, "Forgive us!" He has tenderly invited us to regard Him as our dear Father. In Christ, we know that it is His greatest joy to forgive us and welcome us home. He is the waiting father in Jesus' parable of the prodigal son.

But the father said to his servants, "Bring quickly the

best robe, and put it on him, and put a ring on his hand, and shoes on his feet. And bring the fattened calf and kill it, and let us eat and celebrate. For this my son was dead, and is alive again; he was lost, and is found." So they began to celebrate. (Luke 15:22–24)

We are neither worthy of the things for which we pray, nor have we deserved them.

And so the prodigal confessed, "Father, I have sinned against heaven and before you. I am no longer worthy to be called your son" (Luke 15:21). The hammer of the Law (in the case of the prodigal son, it took eating pig slop before he finally "came to himself" [Luke 15:17]) brings repentance. There is nothing so ingrained in our human psyche as the idea that God is most interested in and rewards merit. It takes a hammer blow to reorient our thinking. "Is not My word like fire, declares the LORD, and like a hammer that breaks the rock in pieces?" (Jeremiah 23:29). The prodigal was finally rendered honest. He deserved nothing from his father. He'd "squandered his property in reckless living" (Luke 15:13). Grace flows downward to the humble, not up to the prideful. "God opposes the proud but gives grace to the humble" (1 Peter 5:5).

We see this reality over and over again in the people with whom Jesus deals in the Gospels. Those who come to Jesus confident of their own uprightness, their own righteousness, only get Law from Jesus. They go away empty-handed, confused, and even angry (Luke 11:37–54; 15; 18). Those who come to Jesus pleading for mercy always receive it from Him (Peter's mother-in-law, Luke 4:38–39; the leper, Luke 5:12; the paralytic, Luke 5:18; the centurion's servant, Luke 7:4; calming the storm, Luke 8:24; Jairus's daughter, Luke 8:41–42, 49–56; the boy with the unclean spirit, Luke 9:38–43; little children, Luke 18:15; the blind beggar, Luke 18:38). Often Jesus intercedes without being asked (the widow's son, Luke 7:12–15; the sinful woman, Luke 7:36–50; the woman with the flow of blood, Luke 8:43–48; Zacchaeus,

Luke 19:1–10). Jesus loves to show mercy to the needy, the unworthy, the unclean, the repentant. He gives only demands and Law to the proud and unrepentant.

But we ask that He would give them all to us by grace,

Grace is all gift. I am "justified by His grace as a gift, through the redemption that is in Christ Jesus" (Romans 3:24). Because God Himself bids me pray, "Forgive us our trespasses," and because my forgiveness depends not one iota on anything in me—any works I do, good intentions, or any feelings I can muster—but only on Christ's merit, God bids me be bold! Christ came for sinners and *only* for sinners! "And as He reclined at table in his [Matthew's] house, many tax collectors and sinners were reclining with Jesus and His disciples, for there were many who followed Him" (Mark 2:15).

. . . for we daily sin much

God, grant me honest recognition of this fact!

> If anyone wants to boast of his godliness and despise others, that person is to think about himself and place his prayer before his eyes. He will find that he is no better than others [Romans 12:3] and that in God's presence all must tuck their tails and be glad that they can gain forgiveness. (LC III 90)

. . . and surely deserve nothing but punishment.

Dear God, help me ever to recognize this bald fact about myself. Grant that I always take Your Law seriously! Under the Law, "none is righteous, no, not one" (Romans 3:10). May I die with the "last thoughts" of Luther on my lips: "We are beggars. That is true" (AE 54:476). "The saying is trustworthy and deserving of full acceptance, that Christ Jesus came into the world to save sinners, of whom I am the foremost" (1 Timothy 1:15).

So we too will sincerely forgive and gladly do good to those who sin against us.

But does not this Fifth Petition come with a proviso? ". . . as we forgive those who trespass against us." Is Jesus telling us we shall be forgiven but only if we first fulfill the condition of forgiving others? No. The forgiveness of Christ is proffered by Him in the Gospel and Sacraments and believed by us. Just as the good tree produces good fruit, so Christ forgives us our sins by the Gospel, and we produce good fruit. Faith then works. The fruit/works do not get us into heaven. But a person rendered forgiven cannot but forgive.

The Large Catechism teaches us that the fact that we forgive is a sure sign and consolation that we have been forgiven and believe it (LC III 96). And it's joyous. "This sign can serve to confirm our consciences and cause them to rejoice" (LC III 98). This does mean that a Christian takes seriously his or her divinely given mandate to forgive others. Where such forgiveness cannot be spoken because of death or distance or destroyed relationships, it should be prayed before God. "Dear God, You have forgiven me. I forgive so-and-so." God, help me speak forgiveness whenever I have opportunity! Help me speak it in my family! A child may indeed have to suffer consequences for improper actions. But help me, dear Lord, to speak forgiveness! Your forgiveness! "I forgive you!"

Finally, this petition is God's own remedy for my bad conscience. Sin nags at my conscience. God has created the conscience to bear witness to the truth of the Law (Romans 2:15). A conscience burdened with sin seeks to avoid God. "The man and his wife hid themselves from the presence of the Lord God" (Genesis 3:8). By sin "the conscience is thrown into unrest, so that it is afraid of God's wrath and displeasure" (LC III 89). Men make various attempts to mask a bad conscience. They bury themselves in lust or wealth or greed (hardly the sole domain of the rich—some of the greediest people I've ever met were beggars!) or, even worse, self-righteousness. But this petition is God's own remedy for the conscience.

For where the heart is not in a right relationship with God, or cannot take such confidence, it will not dare to pray anymore. Such a confident and joyful heart can spring from nothing else than the certain knowledge of the forgiveness of sin. (LC III 92)

Why am I Joy:fully Lutheran?

Because God Himself tenderly invites me to pray confidently, "Forgive us our trespasses as we forgive those who trespass against us." Forgiveness clears my conscience of the effects of sin, renders me daily a child of God, and creates in me a joyful heart, free, ready, and eager to forgive others. There's no better way to live.

Dear Lord Christ, You **instruct** me in this Fifth Petition that it is Your pleasure to forgive my sins, and You do so continuously, "for I daily sin much and surely deserve nothing but punishment."

Lord, there is no way I could ever begin to sufficiently **thank** You for Your grace. But I, beggar that I am, sinner that I am, humbly bow before You in prayerful thanksgiving. Instead of what I deserve, You give me grace.

I **confess**, dear Jesus, that I am daily guilty of all sins of action. The vile things I do not do, I speak. And the vile things I do not speak, I think in thoughts viler still.

Lord, have mercy. Christ, have mercy. Lord, have mercy. Grant that I daily recognize my sin and run to Your forgiveness in the Gospel. Cleanse and renew my conscience. Give me joy. And give me strength and courage to forgive others even as I seek forgiveness from them. Amen.

CHAPTER 21

The Sixth Petition
And lead us not into temptation.

What does this mean? God tempts no one. We pray in this petition that God would guard and keep us so that the devil, the world, and our sinful nature may not deceive us or mislead us into false belief, despair, and other great shame and vice. Although we are attacked by these things, we pray that we may finally overcome them and win the victory.

Count it all joy, my brothers, when you meet trials of various kinds. **(JAMES 1:2)**

What does this mean? God tempts no one.

This is a profound and mysterious truth. Jesus Himself said, "It is necessary that temptations come" (Matthew 18:7). What James wrote is true: "Let no one say when he is tempted, 'I am being tempted by God,' for God cannot be tempted with evil, and He Himself tempts no one" (James 1:13). Jesus had to be tempted by the devil. Why? "For we do not have a high priest who is unable to sympathize with our weaknesses, but one who in every respect has been tempted as we are, yet without sin" (Hebrews 4:15). Jesus suffered everything we sinners suffer. And He overcame all for us in our place. God is not the author of sin or evil. Yet the temptations we face are themselves not outside of His providential care. "God in His purpose has ordained before the time of the world by what crosses and sufferings He would conform every one of His elect to the image of His Son. His cross shall and must work together for good for everyone, because they are called according to God's purpose" (FC SD 11 49).

We pray in this petition that God would guard and keep us

Jesus wants us to pray in the face of temptations. "And when He came to the place, He said to them, 'Pray that you may not enter into temptation'" (Luke 22:40). It is God's holy and blessed will to keep us in faith in the face of all difficulties. He bids us pray specifically for this, and because He has so commanded us, we can have supreme confidence in His merciful care.

. . . so that the devil,

By myself, I'm not up to fighting the devil. He is far too powerful and wily for me.

> If you try to help yourself by your own thoughts and counsel, you will only make the matter worse and give the devil more space. For he has a serpent's head. If it finds an opening into which it can slip, the whole body will follow without stopping. But prayer can prevent him and drive him back. (LC III 111)

But You, Jesus, stood against all the devil could muster and won the victory. "And when the devil had ended every temptation, he departed from Him until an opportune time" (Luke 4:13).

. . . the world,

I shudder to think of the world's power standing against me and all the Church. What Luther wrote in the Large Catechism five centuries ago describes the very world we face today.

> Next comes the world, which offends us in word and deed. It drives us to anger and impatience. In short, there is nothing but hatred and envy, hostility, violence and wrong, unfaithfulness, vengeance, cursing, railing, slander, pride and haughtiness, with useless finery, honor, fame, and power. No one is willing to be the least. Everyone desires to sit at the head of the group and to be seen before all. (LC III 103)

But I cling to You, Jesus. "Woe to the world for temptations to sin! For it is necessary that temptations come, but woe to the one by whom the temptation comes!" (Matthew 18:7). Temptations had to and have to come. You faced the temptation of all the horror of the world and its powers and yet obtained the victory—for me.

. . . and our sinful nature may not deceive us or mislead us into false belief, despair, and other great shame and vice.

> For we dwell in the flesh and carry the old Adam about our neck. He exerts himself and encourages us daily to unchastity, laziness, gluttony and drunkenness, greed and deception, to defraud our neighbor and to overcharge him. In short, the old Adam encourages us to have all kinds of evil lusts, which cling to us by nature and to which we are moved by the society, the example, and what we hear and see of other people. They often wound and inflame even an innocent heart. (LC III 102)

The Scriptures warn again and again about the sinful flesh that is still "hanging around our necks" (AE 22:177). They warn me about desire for wealth. "But those who desire to be rich fall into temptation, into a snare, into many senseless and harmful desires that plunge people into ruin and destruction" (1 Timothy 6:9). They warn me about the temptations of lust and direct me to its remedy. "But because of the temptation to sexual immorality, each man should have his own wife and each woman her own husband" (1 Corinthians 7:2). You, Jesus, spoke the truth about me when You addressed Your disciples, "Watch and pray that you may not enter into temptation. The spirit indeed is willing, but the flesh is weak" (Matthew 26:41). And Your blessed apostle Paul warns me against spiritual pride and smugness: "Brothers, if anyone is caught in any transgression, you who are spiritual should restore him in a spirit of gentleness. Keep watch on yourself, lest you too be tempted" (Galatians 6:1).

Although we are attacked by these things, we pray that we may finally overcome them and win the victory.

At Your direction, O Lord, I pray. The devil, the world, and my flesh are on constant attack. Every moment I feel the desires of the flesh. Every moment the world presses me hard. Every second of the day the devil plots my demise. I pray this Sixth Petition when I start the day. I pray it during the day. I pray it before I lay down at night. I pray it amid every trial and temptation. You are my only hope. "Lord, to whom shall . . . [I] go? You have the words of eternal life" (John 6:68).

So there is no help or comfort except to run here, take hold of the Lord's Prayer, and speak to God from the heart like this: "Dear Father, You have asked me to pray. Don't let me fall because of temptations." Then you will see that the temptations must stop and finally confess themselves conquered. (LC III 110)

Why am I Joy:fully Lutheran?

I am Joy:fully Lutheran because God Himself is my bulwark in the midst of all temptation. I rejoice because I believe what the apostle Peter wrote:

Blessed be the God and Father of our Lord Jesus Christ! According to His great mercy, He has caused us to be born again to a living hope through the resurrection of Jesus Christ from the dead, to an inheritance that is imperishable, undefiled, and unfading, kept in heaven for you, who by God's power are being guarded through faith for a salvation ready to be revealed in the last time. In this you rejoice, though now for a little while, if necessary, you have been grieved by various trials, so that the tested genuineness of your faith—more precious than gold that perishes though it is tested by fire—may be found to result in praise and glory and honor at the revelation of Jesus Christ. (1 Peter 1:3–7)

Almighty and merciful God, You **instruct** me that my enemies, the devil, the world, and my flesh are gruesome and seek my downfall. As a Christian, I am to be aware of this constant threat. You have given me life, salvation, and joy in Your only Son, my Lord Christ, and He invites me to pray in the face of all temptation and promises to hear and answer my prayers.

Dear Father in heaven, I **thank** You for the gift of prayer and specifically for protection in the face of temptation.

O Lord, I **confess** that Satan has gotten the best of me all too often, that the world has misled me, and that my flesh all too often overcomes me and causes me to sin.

Lord, have mercy on me. Lead me not into temptation. Preserve me in the face of all attacks. Give me a heart ever ready to repent and look to You in deep trust. Give to me and all believers at last the victory in time and eternity. Amen!

CHAPTER 22

The Seventh Petition
But deliver us from evil.

> *What does this mean?* We pray in this petition, in summary, that our Father in heaven would rescue us from every evil of body and soul, possessions and reputation, and finally, when our last hour comes, give us a blessed end, and graciously take us from this valley of sorrow to Himself in heaven.

Sing for joy, O heavens, and exult, O earth;
break forth, O mountains, into singing!

For the LORD has comforted His people and will
have compassion on His afflicted. **(ISAIAH 49:13)**

What does this mean? We pray in this petition, in summary, that our Father in heaven would rescue us from every evil of body

In the Western Church, we have prayed, "But deliver us from evil." The Eastern Church prays, "But deliver us from the evil one." Luther combined both and translated the text in such a way that it included both (see Peters, *Lord's Prayer*, 173–75). But in the Large Catechism, Luther leads with the devil as the first enemy: "The entire substance of all our prayer is directed against our chief enemy" (LC III 113). But he immediately broadens the petition: "Dear Father, grant that we be rid of all these disasters" (LC III 114).

. . . and soul,

"What does it profit a man to gain the whole world and forfeit his soul?" (Mark 8:36). The greatest evil of all—and this is the chief endeavor of the devil—is that a person die not knowing the all-encompassing love of the Father, demonstrated in sending His Son for the salvation of all people, "that by believing . . . [they] might have life in His name" (John 20:31). "There is no other name under heaven given among men by which we must be saved" (Acts 4:12). "I am the way, and the truth, and the life. No one comes to the Father except through Me" (John 14:6).

. . . possessions

It is true, there are many warnings in the Bible about the improper love of possessions. I think of the man who built barn after barn to shelter his wealth. "But God said to him, 'Fool! This night your soul is required of you, and the things you have prepared, whose will they be?'" (Luke 12:20). However, there are a plenitude of passages in the Scriptures that tell us wealth is a blessing from God, a result of hard work, and is to be used to benefit others. I know as a Lutheran that the First Article of the Creed is a fulsome, full-throated affirmation of God's wonderful creation. It is "the *love* of money [that] is the root of all kinds of evil," not money itself (1 Timothy 6:10; emphasis added). And even more wonderful is the fact that in God's economy the more we share of our possessions, the more He increases them. "For God loves a cheerful giver. And God is able to make all grace abound to you, so that having all sufficiency in all things at all times, you may abound in every good work" (2 Corinthians 9:7–8).

. . . and reputation,

I shudder when I contemplate the exponential increase of sin and evil visited on this world by the internet. In addition to the sexual filth that so easily entraps, there are the truly horrid violations of the Eighth Commandment. This is a frightening and evil sin, especially in the church and among Christians. Strike hard, O Lord, against my hardened conscience should I be a source of evil, uncharitable, impatient, harsh, and unloving accusations of others. Defend, O Lord, the reputation of the faithful. Cause me and all in the church to be the source of goodness, kindness, and fairmindedness when we speak to and with other Christians and when we interact with nonbelievers.

Rejoice in the Lord always; again I will say, rejoice. Let your reasonableness be known to everyone. The Lord is at hand; do not be anxious about anything, but in everything by prayer and supplication with thanksgiving let your requests be made known to God. And the peace of God, which surpasses all understanding, will guard your hearts and your minds in Christ Jesus.

Finally, brothers, whatever is true, whatever is honorable, whatever is just, whatever is pure, whatever is lovely, whatever is commendable, if there is any excellence, if there is anything worthy of praise, think about these things. What you have learned and received and heard and seen in me—practice these things, and the God of peace will be with you. (Philippians 4:4–9)

. . . and finally, when our last hour comes, give us a blessed end, and graciously take us from this valley of sorrow to Himself in heaven.

Lord, teach me to number my days that I may "get a heart of wisdom" (Psalm 90:12). My end on this earth is coming. You, Lord, know the hour. "My times are in Your hand; rescue me from the hand of my enemies and from my persecutors!" (Psalm 31:15). Sustain me in my Baptism against all assaults of the evil one. Grant me a repentant heart and faith through the hour of my death. Sustain me with Your body and blood until I shall feast with You and all the saints in eternity. At the last, give me Jesus, only Jesus.

Why am I Joy:fully Lutheran?

I am Joy:fully Lutheran because in Jesus I am delivered from the evil one for time and eternity. "For You have been my help, and in the shadow of Your wings I will sing for joy" (Psalm 63:7).

Gracious Savior, in this petition You urge me to pray for protection against all evil, including the devil. And You **instruct** me how to pray for this protection.

I **thank** You, my merciful Redeemer, that You have made Yourself known to me and promise me and all believers in You victory at the last.

I **confess**, Holy Lord, that often I have not fled from the evil one and into Your arms in prayer. I have even run toward his false and cold, deceptive embrace. Forgive me, Lord. Deliver me from the evil one.

Lord, I come with nothing. You have given me everything. Thwart evil in my life. Strengthen me for good. Forgive my countless debt of sins, and plunge that debt into Your infinite, precious, and merciful wounds that I, too, may say at last, "Into Your hands I commit my spirit!" (Luke 23:46; Psalm 31:5). Amen.

CHAPTER 23

THE CONCLUSION
For Thine is the kingdom and the power and the glory forever and ever.* Amen.

> *What does this mean?* This means that I should be certain that these petitions are pleasing to our Father in heaven, and are heard by Him; for He Himself has commanded us to pray in this way and has promised to hear us. Amen, amen means "yes, yes, it shall be so."

*These words were not in Luther's Small Catechism.

For all the promises of God find their Yes in Him. That is why it is through Him that we utter our Amen to God for His glory. **(2 CORINTHIANS 1:20)**

What does this mean? This means that I should be certain that these petitions are pleasing to our Father in heaven.

The entire matter of the Christian faith, and especially so when it comes to the teachings of the Small Catechism, is a matter of absolute certainty. If eternal life is something I acquire whole or in part by my deeds, then certainty is not possible. In fact, if I am hoping that my good deeds outweigh the bad, or if I'm hoping that after hundreds of thousands of years in an alleged purgatory, I have suffered enough punishments to finally be pure enough to get to heaven, certainty seems like arrogance. If I'm honest, I recognize I'm far from perfect and I may hope that God will receive me. But that remains to be seen. This is not the faith of the Bible.

God has granted absolute certainty in the matter of eternal life, and in fact, in all matters of Christianity. "If you abide in My word, you are truly My disciples, and you will know the truth, and the truth will set you free" (John 8:31–32). "And this is eternal life, that they know You, the only true God, and Jesus Christ whom You have sent" (John 17:3). The Bible is written so that I may have certainty about Christ and eternal life. The apostle John wrote at the end of his Gospel, "But these are written so that you may believe that Jesus is the Christ, the Son of God, and that by believing you may have life in His name" (John 20:31). Paul's writings are filled with such certainty.

> But whatever gain I had, I counted as loss for the sake of Christ. Indeed, I count everything as loss because of the surpassing worth of knowing Christ Jesus my Lord. For His sake I have suffered the loss of all things and count them as rubbish, in order that I may gain Christ and be found in Him, not having a righteousness of my own that comes from the law, but that which comes through faith in Christ, the righteousness from God that depends on faith. (Philippians 3:7–9)

And the apostle Paul specifically enjoins believers to imitate his certainty in Christ.

> But I am not ashamed, for I know whom I have believed, and I am convinced that He is able to guard until that day what has been entrusted to me. Follow the pattern of the sound words that you have heard from me, in the faith and love that are in Christ Jesus. By the Holy Spirit who dwells within us, guard the good deposit entrusted to you. (2 Timothy 1:12–14)

Certainty is possible because eternal life depends upon Christ, not me. I am uncertain. My decisions vacillate. My piety wanes. My zeal for the Word of God fluctuates. My sinful flesh grabs me and presses hard against me from time to time. I break my resolutions. I forget my promises. I resolve to follow Jesus more seriously, only to be dashed by sin, death, and devil. "Wretched man that I am! Who will deliver me from this body of death? Thanks be to God through Jesus Christ our Lord!" (Romans 7:24–25). "You did not choose Me, but I chose you," Jesus told the disciples (John 15:16).

I am certain of eternal life, and I am certain that God hears my prayers because of Jesus; Jesus' conception for me; Jesus' sinless birth for me; Jesus' perfect childhood for me; Jesus' Baptism for me; Jesus' temptation for me; Jesus' healing and preaching for me; Jesus' instituting the Supper for me; Jesus' bloody sweat in the garden for me; Jesus' betrayal by Judas for me; Jesus' trial and ridicule before Pilate and Herod for me; His flogging for me; His ridicule and suffering blows from the soldiers for me; His carrying his cross for me; His nails for me; His glorious words from the cross for me; "Father, forgive them" for me (Luke 23:34); "Today you will be with Me in paradise," (Luke 23:43) for me; "It is finished" for me (John 19:30); His death for me; His burial for me; His descent to proclaim victory in hell for me; His resurrection for me; His ascension to the right hand of the Father for me!

All this for me! Wretched worm that I am. The Father has counted me as precious as the blood of God in the flesh (Acts 20:28). And after all this, He bids me pray to Him. "Amen."

. . . and are heard by Him; for He Himself has commanded us to pray in this way and has promised to hear us.

And when you pray, you must not be like the hypocrites. For they love to stand and pray in the synagogues and at the street corners, that they may be seen by others. Truly, I say to you, they have received their reward. But when you pray, go into your room and shut the door and pray to your Father who is in secret. And your Father who sees in secret will reward you. (Matthew 6:5–6)

Amen, amen means "yes, yes, it shall be so."

Amen. I believe it.

WHY AM I JOY:FULLY LUTHERAN?

I am joyful because looking away from myself and my unending weakness, I have full assurance and confidence in Christ that I am God's own dear child. And because He has taught me how to pray, and in Christ's name, He hears and answers my prayers.

Holy and righteous Father, You **instruct** me in the conclusion to the prayer taught by Your beloved Son to have full confidence in You as I pray. I know You will answer my prayer exactly for my benefit and the benefit of those for whom I pray.

Father, I **thank** You for the certainty to say "Amen! It shall be so!" I pray it knowing I am declared righteous and forgiven by You and that heaven is mine.

I **confess**, dear Father in heaven, that I have wavered. I have doubted Your goodness. I have doubted Your will. I have complained about Your fatherly chastisement. I have prayed many a half-hearted "Amen."

Restore me, O Lord. Grant me apostolic certainty in the life and death and resurrection of Jesus! Grant me certainty in Baptism, Absolution, and the Lord's Supper! Grant me a round, full, faithful "Amen" to Your will, come what may. At my last breath, grant me an audible "Amen," as testimony to You and to my loved ones, witnessing to Your unending grace to me a sinner. Amen! Yea, yea! It shall be so!

The Sacrament of Holy Baptism

As the head of the family should teach it
in a simple way to his household

First
What is Baptism?

> Baptism is not just plain water, but it is the water included in God's command and combined with God's word.

Which is that word of God?

> Christ our Lord says in the last chapter of Matthew: "Therefore go and make disciples of all nations, baptizing them in the name of the Father and of the Son and of the Holy Spirit." (Matthew 28:19)

The name of the LORD is a strong tower;
the righteous man runs into it and is safe.
(PROVERBS 18:10)

Baptism is not just plain water,

I am baptized. Bethel Lutheran Church in Lawton, Iowa, has a record of my Baptism taking place on April 15, 1962. As of this writing, the pastor who performed the act is living. I've spoken to him. My parents are alive and have given me details. My sponsors, Aunt Annette and Uncle Bill, are alive to tell of it. I have a certificate assuring that it happened. Baptism is something special. That's why we make sure it is verifiable. An uncertain Baptism must be regarded as no Baptism. Baptism exists for certainty. This is because it is "not just plain water." If Baptism were my action to demonstrate that I'm serious about Jesus or repentance, or if Baptism were my voluntary participation in a symbolic action that represents cleansing of sin or rebirth or committing my life to Jesus, then "just plain water" would do.

In Jesus' own Baptism, we get a very powerful first look at this unique washing, and we note something special is going on.

Then Jesus came from Galilee to the Jordan to John, to be baptized by him. John would have prevented Him, saying, "I need to be baptized by You, and do You come to me?" But Jesus answered him, "Let it be so now, for thus it is fitting for us to fulfill all righteousness." Then he consented. And when Jesus was baptized, immediately He went up from the water, and behold, the heavens were opened to Him, and He saw the Spirit of God descending like a dove and coming to rest on Him; and behold, a voice from heaven said, "This is My beloved Son, with whom I am well pleased." (Matthew 3:13–17)

First, John the Baptizer wanted to prevent Jesus' Baptism. Why in the world would Jesus, whom John called the sinless "Lamb of God who takes away the sin of the world," need to be baptized? He did not need to be baptized for Himself. But He was baptized for me. "Let it be," said Jesus. "It is fitting to fulfill all righteousness." Jesus let Himself be baptized as though He were a common sinner just like me. In doing so, He Himself created my path to eternal life, through water. And not just "plain water."

. . . but it is the water included in God's command

"It is fitting." That is, God the Father, in fact the entire Holy Trinity, mandated it for Jesus. God's mandate cannot be meaningless. Because of the way Jesus' Baptism transpires, I recognize that Baptism is not about symbols or showing God how serious I am about following Him. It is not my action. It is divine action. In Jesus' Baptism is given the most extraordinary epiphany of the triune God. Jesus "sticks Himself in the water" (Luther). The Spirit of God descends from heaven to rest on Him. And the Father from heaven speaks, "This is My beloved Son, with whom I am well pleased" (Matthew 3:17).

. . . and combined with God's word.

The Word of God, which recounts Jesus' Baptism, shows us the Trinity is in action in Baptism. The Son acts in our stead, for us, "fulfilling all righteousness." "Jesus sticks Himself in the water so that when we go into the water we come out with Him" (Luther). In Baptism, heaven is open! "Behold, the heavens were opened to Him." In Baptism, the Father speaks. "This is My beloved." In Baptism, the Spirit descends. Moreover, the specific command and Word of God to be combined with the water is given to us by Jesus.

> So, and even much more, you must honor Baptism and consider it glorious because of the Word. For God Himself has honored it both by words and deeds. Furthermore, He confirmed it with miracles from heaven. Do you think it was a joke that, when Christ was baptized, the heavens were opened and the Holy Spirit descended visibly, and everything was divine glory and majesty [Luke 3:21–22]? (LC IV 21)

Christ our Lord says in the last chapter of Matthew:

The Father Himself bids us, "Listen to Him [Christ]!" (Luke 9:35). Christ the Lord Himself, after His resurrection and before His ascension, left the Church His baptismal mandate.

"Therefore go and make disciples of all nations,

The text actually says, "As you are going." The church, Christians, pastors are going. And going, disciples are made. A disciple follows Jesus. "Lord, to whom shall we go? You have the words of eternal life" (John 6:68). "If anyone would come after Me, let him deny himself and take up his cross and follow Me. For whoever would save his life will lose it, but whoever loses his life for My sake will find it" (Matthew 16:24–25). And disciples come from "all nations." There is no room for racial discrimination in the church. End of story.

. . . baptizing them

How are disciples made? By baptizing them. Who? "All nations." Where shall this message of Jesus and His Baptism be taken? "All nations." Who shall be baptized? "All nations." Who is excluded from this promise? No one. No adult. No sinner. No malefactor. No male. No female. No child. No infant. Jesus simply says, "All nations are made disciples by baptizing them." Baptism is not an option in the church's life and mission.

. . . in the name of the Father and of the Son and of the Holy Spirit." (Matthew 28:19)

The Lord Himself has taught us in the First Petition of the Lord's Prayer that we do not mess with His name. "You shall not take the name of the LORD your God in vain, for the LORD will not hold him guiltless who takes His name in vain" (Exodus 20:7). Because God's Word and name are combined with this water, "it is nothing other than a divine water" (LC IV 14). "To be baptized in God's name is to be baptized not by men, but by God Himself. Therefore, although it is performed by human hands, it is still truly God's own work" (LC IV 10).

Why am I Joy:fully Lutheran?

Because I am baptized. The Baptism of Christ shows its glory and benefits (an open heaven!). In Christ, the Father says to me, "This is My beloved." My own Baptism is mandated by Christ and pleasing to Him.

Holy Trinity, through the account of the Baptism of Jesus, You **instruct** me that Baptism is a glorious and divine gift, pleasing to You. You, Father, speak Your blessing. You, Christ, take my place in the water. You, Holy Spirit, descend on the Son.

Almighty God, I **thank** You that I am baptized and that Your most holy name is placed on me by divine mandate and action! The pastor's hands and mouth that poured water and spoke Your name on me so long ago were Your hands and mouth. "So it is nothing other than a divine water" (LC IV 14).

I **confess**, O Lord, my failure to treasure my Baptism. "Every Christian has enough in Baptism to learn and to do all his life" (LC IV 41). Yet I so very often ignore the many promises connected to Baptism in the Scriptures. I despise my Baptism, against which I sin willfully. I am callous and careless every moment I fail to repent and return to Baptism's blessings.

O Father, Son, and Holy Spirit! You have made me Your own! Suffer me not to my own devices! Leave me not! Humble me however You choose. Bring cross and trial as You will. Only drive me to cling to Your holy name in Baptism. Amen.

CHAPTER 25

SECOND

What benefits does Baptism give?

It works forgiveness of sins, rescues from death and the devil, and gives eternal salvation to all who believe this, as the words and promises of God declare

Which are these words and promises of God?

Christ our Lord says in the last chapter of Mark: "Whoever believes and is baptized will be saved, but whoever does not believe will be condemned." (Mark 16:16)

Wash me thoroughly from my iniquity,
and cleanse me from my sin! (PSALM 51:2)

What benefits does Baptism give?

The Large Catechism answers this question in a very profound way. "When our sins and conscience oppress us, we strengthen ourselves and take comfort and say, 'Nevertheless, I am baptized. And if I am baptized, it is promised to me that I shall be saved and have eternal life, both in soul and body'" (LC IV 44). This is because Baptism is the forgiveness of sins. It rescues from sin, death, and the devil. In fact, Baptism *is* the Gospel.

It works forgiveness of sins,

"Repent and *be baptized every one of you in the name of Jesus Christ for the forgiveness of your sins*, and you will receive the gift of the Holy Spirit" (Acts 2:38; emphasis added). The texts of the New Testament dealing with Baptism are shocking. The Platonist in each of us wants to separate the spiritual from the physical. This forever confounds well-meaning Christians. God has given me His written, inspired, and inerrant Word. Yet I forever want to separate God's "will" or intention for my life from the actual, express written words that God has given. "Did God really say . . . ?" (Genesis 3:1). God has given His own Son into death, raised Him from the dead, and given very clear words through this Christ and His chosen apostles about the exclusivity of the Gospel. "There is no other name under heaven given among men by which we must be saved" (Acts 4:12). Yet my reason asks: "Won't God save those who don't know Christ?" God through Christ gave us the apostolic Office of the Ministry; the apostles appointed pastors, evangelists, and teachers to continue this office. In Paul's Pastoral Epistles, we are told repeatedly what the task of the Office of the Ministry is: to preach the Word and administer the Sacraments as God's own ambassadors.[3] St. Paul even says the Office of the Ministry is for our joy! "Not that we lord it over your faith, *but we work with you for your joy*, for you stand firm in your faith" (2 Corinthians 1:24; emphasis added).

Yet my flesh causes me to question God's gift and order and office, such that I ask: Do I really need to go to church to be a Christian? Must I have a pastor to preach the Gospel to me? Do I really need the church for my sins to be forgiven? God is un-

---

3   Note what the great second-generation Lutheran Martin Chemnitz (1522–86), driving force behind the Book of Concord (1580), says about pastors. "Paul commands Timothy and Titus to entrust the ministry to faithful and able men. 2 Timothy 2:2; 3:2; Titus 1:9" (Chemnitz 28). It is certainly true that all Christians are spiritual priests and enjoy the full privileges of this priesthood. But Christ also instituted the Office of the Ministry. As Chemnitz wrote, "All Christians have a general call to proclaim the Gospel of God, Romans 10:9, to speak the Word of God among themselves, Ephesians 5:19; to admonish each other from the Word of God . . . ; to reprove, Ephesians 5:11 [and] Matthew 19:15; [and] to comfort, 1 Thessalonians 4:18. And family heads are enjoined [to do] this with the special command that they give their households the instruction of the Lord. Ephesians 6:4. But the public ministry of the Word and of the Sacraments in the church is not entrusted to all Christians in general, as we have already shown, 1 Corinthians 12:28; Ephesians 4:12. For a special or particular call is required for this, Romans 10:15" (Chemnitz 29; brackets in original).

imaginably generous with His Gospel and desires His Gospel to be delivered to me at church, through Word and Sacrament (Hebrews 10:25). He has made me and all Christians spiritual priests who are to speak Christ and His forgiveness and to receive such forgiveness spoken in our vocations and homes (1 Peter 2:9). Yet it is our propensity to avoid speaking the Gospel to others and receiving the Gospel from others, even in our own families! He gives us pastors to give us the Sacrament of the Altar for absolute assurance of forgiveness that we might have a good conscience before Him (1 Corinthians 4:1; Hebrews 10:19–24). Yet we run from these concrete means—ways and gifts for forgiveness—and we regress into our own minds or too often into supposedly lofty thoughts about how and when and where God works, which have not the slightest promise of God's forgiveness! Baptism works forgiveness of sins!

. . . rescues from death

Baptism rescues from death! St. Paul held forth a list of sins under the nose of the Corinthians. But then he notes the very concrete remedy for such sin: "washing."

> Or do you not know that the unrighteous will not inherit the kingdom of God? Do not be deceived: neither the sexually immoral, nor idolaters, nor adulterers, nor men who practice homosexuality, nor thieves, nor the greedy, nor drunkards, nor revilers, nor swindlers will inherit the kingdom of God. And such were some of you. *But you were washed, you were sanctified, you were justified in the name of the Lord Jesus Christ and by the Spirit of our God.* (1 Corinthians 6:9–11; emphasis added)

Baptism changed everything for them! They were "washed." And by such washing of Baptism, they were "sanctified," that is, made holy ones, because of Jesus' holiness given in Baptism. By such washing, they were "justified." That is, they were declared "not guilty" for the sake of Jesus in Baptism (as we shall note in Titus 3)!

In fact, Baptism is described in the New Testament as a movement from death to life. This is not because Baptism is a symbolic act that buries us in water like Christ was buried in the tomb. Baptism is a real dying and rising with Christ because in Baptism we are connected with Jesus! All that is His becomes ours! Baptism really connects us with Jesus' death and its benefits. Baptism really forgives our sins and makes us alive. Because it connects us with Jesus, it promises not only that I shall live beyond the grave but also that I—this very body and soul—shall rise with Christ from death to eternal life!

> Do you not know that all of us who have been baptized into Christ Jesus were baptized into His death? We were buried therefore with Him by baptism into death, in order that, just as Christ was raised from the dead by the glory of the Father, we too might walk in newness of life. (Romans 6:3–4)

. . . and the devil,

The gift of divine sonship rescues from the devil. The devil hates Baptism. He works overtime to turn the Gospel of Baptism into a work that we do. He would rob the treasure from us and leave us with a bad conscience, looking for knowledge of God's will and purpose for our lives anywhere but in the very place where God has given us all we need: Baptism!

. . . and gives eternal salvation

St. Peter could not have said it any clearer:

> For Christ also suffered once for sins, the righteous for the unrighteous, that He might bring us to God, being put to death in the flesh but made alive in the spirit, in which He went and proclaimed to the spirits in prison, because they formerly did not obey, when God's patience waited in the days of Noah, while the ark was being prepared, in which a few, that is, eight persons, were brought safely through water. *Baptism, which cor-*

responds to this, now saves you, not as a removal of dirt from the body but as an appeal to God for a good conscience, through the resurrection of Jesus Christ, who has gone into heaven and is at the right hand of God, with angels, authorities, and powers having been subjected to Him. (1 Peter 3:18–22; emphasis added)

Just as does St. Paul, so St. Peter says the benefits of Christ's suffering, death, and resurrection were accomplished once for all. And those benefits are delivered to us in Baptism. How is this? It is because Baptism saves by connecting us to the resurrection of Christ. The blessings of Christ's resurrection are ours. Baptism saves just like the ark saved eight people from the worldwide flood (Genesis 6–9). Baptism saves not by washing dirt from the body "but as an appeal to God for a good conscience" (1 Peter 3:21)! Don't be fooled by the devil's sleight of hand. *The "appeal" is not something we do.* The appeal is not *my* action or request to God. *The "appeal" is Baptism itself.* My conscience is clear because my debt is paid. I am a sinner to be sure; I shall struggle with sin throughout my Christian life. But I am acquitted. God loves me and accepts me in Jesus, in my Baptism.

. . . to all who believe this,

The treasure was attained at the cross and in the resurrection of Jesus. The treasure is doled out in Baptism, Absolution, the Word of the Gospel, and the Lord's Supper. Faith lays hold of it and makes it mine. Only faith. If it's all gift—and it is—then only faith grabs hold of the treasure.

. . . as the words and promises of God declare.

The Bible could not be clearer. St. Paul describes this faith as itself a gift of grace, even as he does so in baptismal language.

But God, being rich in mercy, because of the great love with which He loved us, *even when we were dead in our trespasses, made us alive together with Christ—by grace you have been saved—and raised us up with Him and* seated us with Him in the heavenly places in Christ Jesus, so that in the coming ages He might show the immeasurable riches of His grace in kindness toward us in Christ Jesus. *For by grace you have been saved through faith. And this is not your own doing; it is the gift of God*, not a result of works, so that no one may boast. (Ephesians 2:4–9; emphasis added)

Which are these words and promises of God? Christ our Lord says in the last chapter of Mark: "Whoever believes and is baptized will be saved,

This is Gospel. Baptism is, "in short, so full of consolation and grace that heaven and earth cannot understand it. But it requires skill to believe this, for the treasure is not lacking, but this is lacking: people who grasp it and hold it firmly" (LC IV 39–40). Faith receives the treasure. Where faith fails, or walks away from the blessings, Baptism still holds good. God beckons us repent, return, and again lay hold of the gift, which is accomplished and firm.

. . . but whoever does not believe will be condemned." (Mark 16:16)

This is Law. The Law threatens death and damnation, but always for a purpose: repentance and faith.

WHY AM I JOY:FULLY LUTHERAN?

I am Joy:fully Lutheran because all of Christ's benefits are mine in my Baptism. It is objective fact that God has chosen me for eternal life. He brought His eternal desire for my salvation to reality in me at a font by the hands of a pastor, by water and Word. He's put His own most holy name on me. He has granted me faith to receive it. It is beyond all doubt. My conscience is clear. I am His. He is mine.

Lord of all mercy and grace, You have **instructed** me by Your clearest Word that Baptism is replete with the greatest of temporal and eternal blessings.

Lord of all consolation for the troubled conscience, I **thank** You that I am baptized and have forgiveness and surety of eternal life in my Baptism.

I **confess**, holy God, that I have neglected Your Word, especially the great teachings that You give me for a life as Your dear, baptized child.

O Lord, by Your own blessed Baptism, grant me daily repentance! Grant that I treasure Your gifts more and more every hour that I live on this earth. And take me to be with You and all Your baptized and believing people at the last. Amen.

CHAPTER 26

THIRD
How can water do such great things?

> Certainly not just water, but the word of God in and with the water does these things, along with the faith which trusts this word of God in the water. For without God's word the water is plain water and no Baptism. But with the word of God it is a Baptism, that is, a life-giving water, rich in grace, and a washing of the new birth in the Holy Spirit, as St. Paul says in Titus, chapter three:

> "He saved us through the washing of rebirth and renewal by the Holy Spirit, whom He poured out on us generously through Jesus Christ our Savior, so that, having been justified by His grace, we might become heirs having the hope of eternal life. This is a trustworthy saying." (Titus 3:5–8)

They shall come and sing aloud on the height of Zion, and they shall be radiant over the goodness of the LORD, over the grain, the wine, and the oil, and over the young of the flock and the herd; their life shall be like a watered garden, and they shall languish no more. **(JEREMIAH 31:12)**

How can water do such great things?

I am by nature, by my sinful nature, what Dr. Luther called a "fanatic" or "enthusiast." He used these words not, as we commonly do, for a person who is very serious about sports or some other avocation. For Luther, the word *fanatic* meant a person who looks for God's Word and will somewhere other than where He has actually given it: in His Word and Sacraments. Dr. Luther put it this way as he tells us this propensity is part of every one of us.

In a word, enthusiasm dwells in Adam and his children from the beginning to the end of the world. Its venom has been implanted and infused into them by the old serpent. It is the origin, power, and strength of all heresy, especially of the papacy and Muhammad. Therefore, we must constantly maintain this point: God does not want to deal with us in any other way than through the spoken Word and the Sacraments. Whatever is praised as from the Spirit—without the Word and Sacraments—is the devil himself. (SA III VIII 9–10)

So my inner fanatic, my old Adam, my flesh, scoffs, "How can water do such great things? How can all the blessings of Christ be tied to a handful of water?"

Certainly not just water,

You fool! You fanatic! You enthusiast! You are staring at the font and Baptism like it were mere water, like any ordinary "dog or cow's bath" (WA 37:642)! "We always teach that the Sacraments and all outward things that God ordains and institutes should not be considered according to the coarse, outward mask, the way we look at a nutshell. But we respect them because God's Word is included in them" (LC IV 19).

. . . but the word of God in and with the water does these things,

St. Augustine got it right sixteen hundred years ago. "When the Word is joined to the element . . . , it becomes a Sacrament" (LC IV 18). The powerful Word of God makes the Baptism. The Word of God stretched forth the universe (John 1:3). God is active precisely through His "living and active" Word (Hebrews 4:12).

He is the living God, acting, speaking, working, striving to make His claim on man. He kills and He makes alive; He exalts and He casts down; He speaks, He gives knowledge, He shows His strength, He performs mercy,

He delivers. He not only loves, but He makes His love manifest by sending His only-begotten Son into the world. He not only hates sin, but He executes judgment, and His wrath is actually revealed from heaven against all ungodliness and unrighteousness of men. God's grace and His justice, His omnipresence and His holiness, His majesty and His glory are not quiescent attributes, but are active and dynamic. And as God is, so is His Word. (Preus, "The Power of God's Word," 105)

Psalm 33:9 is true of Baptism: "For He spoke, and it came to be; He commanded, and it stood firm."

. . . along with the faith which trusts this word of God in the water.

God places His Word and name into the water. His name and Word create faith, particularly in the case of infants. Faith grabs the blessings out of the water.

For without God's word the water is plain water and no Baptism. But with the word of God it is a Baptism, that is, a life-giving water,

Note that Baptism is smack in the center of this passage. "In Him also you were circumcised with a circumcision made without hands, by putting off the body of the flesh, by the circumcision of Christ, *having been buried with Him in baptism,* in which you were also raised with Him through faith in the powerful working of God, who raised Him from the dead. And you, who were dead in your trespasses and the uncircumcision of your flesh, *God made alive together with Him,* having forgiven us all our trespasses, by canceling the record of debt that stood against us with its legal demands. This He set aside, nailing it to the cross" (Colossians 2:11–14; emphasis added). Baptism is the delivery point for eternal life!

. . . rich in grace,

Baptism is all grace according to St. Paul in Ephesians. It's all gift. "Husbands, love your wives, as Christ loved the church and gave Himself up for her, that He might sanctify her, *having cleansed her by the washing of water with the word*, so that He might present the church to Himself in splendor, without spot or wrinkle or any such thing, that she might be holy and without blemish" (Ephesians 5:25–27; emphasis added).

. . . and a washing of the new birth in the Holy Spirit,

Jesus laid it out all very clearly to Nicodemus:

> "Truly, truly, I say to you, unless one is born again he cannot see the kingdom of God." Nicodemus said to Him, "How can a man be born when he is old? Can he enter a second time into his mother's womb and be born?" Jesus answered, *"Truly, truly, I say to you, unless one is born of water and the Spirit, he cannot enter the kingdom of God."* (John 3:3–5; emphasis added)

. . . as St. Paul says in Titus, chapter three: "He saved us through the washing of rebirth and renewal by the Holy Spirit,

The same verse in Titus also says, "He saved us . . . not because of works done by us in righteousness" (3:5).

Baptism is no work done by us. How does Paul say the saving takes place? "Through"—by means of—"the washing," which is in itself a "rebirth and renewal" (using the very words Jesus used with Nicodemus!), "by"—that is, effected by—"the Holy Spirit." Baptism saves. This is the plain, simple, repeated truth of the Bible

. . . whom He poured out on us generously through Jesus Christ our Savior,

When God gives His grace, He gives it in only one way: Generously! Richly! Profusely! And it always comes "through Christ." And where is Christ? In His Word and Sacrament.

. . . so that, having been justified by His grace,

It's the devil's trick to pull this justification (i.e., being declared as in a court of law "not guilty" before God because of Christ) away from the Word and water of Baptism. St. Paul clearly teaches here that Baptism *is* justification.

. . . we might become heirs having the hope of eternal life.

The result of Baptism laid hold of by faith? I am an heir. Heirs receive an inheritance at the grace, generosity, and promise of their benefactor. "And if you are Christ's, then you are Abraham's offspring, heirs according to promise" (Galatians 3:29). Baptism makes it so because it actually connects me to Christ and His benefits.

This is a trustworthy saying." (Titus 3:5–8)

"I *am* baptized!"

Why am I Joy:fully Lutheran?

Because the Bible teaches with crystal clarity that "great things" are done in the water of Baptism. God's Word makes it happen. I am baptized in the name of the Father and of the Son and of the Holy Spirit. All the promises of forgiveness and life and salvation are mine now. Endless profound joy.

Triune God, You have given me the clearest **instruction** on Baptism. Your own inerrant and inspired Word, the words of Jesus, the words of St. Paul, the words of St. Peter, all profess the clear truth that Baptism is Your work, Your gracious saving action.

I **thank** You, Father, Son, and Spirit, that I am baptized.

Holy Trinity, I **confess** that daily I fall short; I have often lived as though I were not baptized at all. I have failed to grasp the treasure that is mine in the water and the Word.

Dearest and most merciful God, restore me! Every time I make the sign of the cross, remind me I am Yours because of a font. Grant me contrition and repentance every day of my life, that I never lose sight of Your promise. "Whoever believes and is baptized will be saved" (Mark 16:16).

CHAPTER 27

Fourth
What does such baptizing with water indicate?

> It indicates that the Old Adam in us should by daily contrition and repentance be drowned and die with all sins and evil desires, and that a new man should daily emerge and arise to live before God in righteousness and purity forever.

Where is this written?

> St. Paul writes in Romans chapter six: "We were therefore buried with Him through baptism into death in order that, just as Christ was raised from the dead through the glory of the Father, we too may live a new life." (Romans 6:4)

Your dead shall live; their bodies shall rise. You who dwell in the dust, awake and sing for joy!
(ISAIAH 26:19)

What does such baptizing with water indicate?

Living one's Baptism is not static. Living life in Christ's forgiveness and mercy is a daily struggle and blessing. As Titus 3 demonstrates so vividly, the verbs that happen to us in Baptism result in a lively dance of faith in this life. Baptism saves. Baptism brings "regeneration" and "renewal." Baptism is "poured out on us generously." Baptism justifies. Baptism is an act of "grace" that endures. Baptism makes living, breathing "heirs." Baptism gives "hope." Baptism gives "eternal life." And all of this is a "trustworthy" saying. That means we live with all these blessings daily and joyously. "Therefore, every Christian has enough in Baptism to learn and to do all his life. For he has always enough to do by believing firmly what Baptism promises and brings: victory over death and the devil [Romans 6:3–6], forgiveness of sin [Acts 2:38], God's grace [Titus 3:5–6], the entire Christ, and the Holy Spirit with His gifts [1 Corinthians 6:11]" (LC IV 41).

It indicates that the Old Adam in us should by daily contrition and repentance be drowned and die

I struggle with the old Adam. He's a persistent monster, even though he's mortally wounded. I think what ought not be thought. I say things that should never cross the lips of a child of God, whether in anger, jealousy, pride, or just plain self-aggrandizing slander. While I have avoided gross outward sins, my flesh still plagues me. Luther says the sins of youth are sexual, the sins of old age, greed. I find such joy in service to Christ and His people, I find such overwhelming joy in loving my family and providing them what is necessary for life, with a home, an education, food and clothing, love. Yet right when I am most humbly serving others, pride puffs me up. Twisted resentment over lack of recognition clouds my vision. I must kneel at my Baptism daily. I must hear the harsh words of the Law daily, to have a mind clear enough to say to God's Law, "Yes. What you say is true. I am a sinner." I must be drowned again and again in the killing and life-giving water of Baptism.

. . . with all sins and evil desires,

I confess them all, dear Christ. Every Commandment broken and broken daily. I feel as though I hang and cling to You by only a thread at times. But just that thread of hope causes me to be honest with myself and, more important, with You, O God. Addicts lie. My sinful flesh is a liar. Addicts obfuscate. Addicts accuse and deny. Addicts hide under a pretext of uprightness. Addicts lie to themselves about their piety. Addicts fume at the supposed addictions of others. Addicts judge. Addicts aggrandize their "good" deeds. Addicts love to be praised. Addicts seethe under a smile when others are recognized and lauded. I confess them all, dear Christ. Drown me every day. Drown me. Kill the old Adam, O Thou new Adam!

. . . and that a new man should daily emerge and arise

It has to be a resurrection. I'm a Lazarus. I'm dead without You, Christ. Forgive me! Cleanse me! Have mercy on me and grant me faith in Your mercy! May the sin that deceives and promises so much gold but delivers short-lived glitter and pleasure and ongoing troubles of conscience become bitter to me! Help me, Savior, for I am about to drown! Yes! Drown me! Raise me to love Your Word, to cherish Your Gospel, to seek Your preached Word and "gladly hear and learn it." I have tasted of the joy of Your salvation! "You prepare a table before me in the presence of my enemies [sin, death, and devil]" (Psalm 23:5). "How sweet are Your words to my taste, sweeter than honey to my mouth!" (Psalm 119:103). I *do* love Your Word, O Christ! I *do* rejoice in the good, O Savior! I *do* love to serve You, O Jesus!

My conscience has troubled me. Whenever I fall to sin, plague my conscience, O Lord, so that I repent and say, "Nevertheless, I am baptized" (LC IV 44). When others sin against me, give me faith to forgive them before You in the Lord's Prayer. Give me courage and kindness to go to my brother or sister. "If your brother sins against you, go and tell him his fault, between you and him alone" (Matthew 18:15). When a brother or sister approaches me about a wrong I have committed, give me humility and open ears. Remind me that You have forgiven me a raft of sins and I cannot but forgive lest I be a hypocrite and reject Your grace and my Baptism. Cleanse my conscience daily in my Baptism. "Let us draw near with a true heart in full assurance of faith, with our hearts sprinkled clean from an evil conscience and our bodies washed with pure water" (Hebrews 10:22). Grant a ready and sincere apology and plea for forgiveness. Grant me peace in family, workplace, and church. Daily strengthen me to live as St. Paul. "So I always take pains to have a clear conscience toward both God and man" (Acts 24:16). This is simply to live in my Baptism.

. . . to live before God in righteousness and purity forever.

In my Baptism, I have nothing less than the righteousness and purity of Christ. I have it now, however much I struggle. And in Baptism, I have the surety of eternal life. "If I am baptized, it is promised to me that I shall be saved and have eternal life, both in soul and body" (LC IV 44).

***Where is this written?* St. Paul writes in Romans chapter six: "We were therefore buried with Him through baptism into death**

The original says we are "buried with Him through baptism into *the* death." Which death? Christ's substitutionary, sacrificial death. Being buried with Christ is reality, not symbolic language. The metaphor is Paul comparing the going into the water and coming out of it to the death and resurrection effected. The Bible mandates water for Baptism, but not how much. And Baptism is described as "washing" and "sprinkled" (Titus 3:5; Hebrews 10:22).

. . . in order that, just as Christ was raised from the dead through the glory of the Father, we too may live a new life." (Romans 6:4)

Having died with Christ, having been connected with His own death in the very waters of Baptism, we now live a new life. How? Christ has bound us together with Him. As Paul continues, "For if we have been united with Him in a death like His, we shall certainly be united with Him in a resurrection like His" (Romans 6:5).

WHY AM I JOY:FULLY LUTHERAN?

I am Joy:fully Lutheran because the new man in me is daily raised, forgiven, and given a clean conscience. Though harassed and harangued by my sin and the sins of others, I am not defined by that sin. I am baptized and I rejoice.

Merciful Lord, You give me the clearest possible **instruction** in Your Word about what Baptism is and does. You **instruct** me to look to my Baptism for consolation, hope, and joy.

Dear Lord, I **thank** You that my parents and sponsors brought me to a font. I **thank** You that a pastor baptized me. I **thank** You that my sinful flesh has been drowned and continues to be daily drowned as I recall my Baptism and cling to You. You have raised me to live anew and for You. And in Baptism, You promise my resurrection.

Gracious God, I **confess** to You all my sins, especially the sin of despising my Baptism by thinking, speaking, and acting as though I were not baptized at all. I'm guilty.

Dearest Savior, forgive my sins. Grant that I treasure Your gift of Baptism. Let me never be severed from You. Cause me to be an advocate and messenger, that "all nations" become Your disciples through Baptism for eternal life. Amen.

CONFESSION

How Christians should be taught to confess

CHAPTER 28

Confession
What is Confession?

> Confession has two parts. First, that we confess our sins, and second, that we receive absolution, that is, forgiveness, from the pastor as from God Himself, not doubting, but firmly believing that by it our sins are forgiven before God in heaven.

What sins should we confess?

> Before God we should plead guilty of all sins, even those we are not aware of, as we do in the Lord's Prayer; but before the pastor we should confess only those sins which we know and feel in our hearts.

Which are these?

> Consider your place in life according to the Ten Commandments: Are you a father, mother, son, daughter, husband, wife, or worker? Have you been disobedient, unfaithful, or lazy? Have you been hot-tempered, rude, or quarrelsome? Have you hurt someone by your words or deeds? Have you stolen, been negligent, wasted anything, or done any harm?

Take heart, My son; your sins are forgiven.
(MATTHEW 9:2)

What is Confession?

There are three distinct uses of the word *confession* in the New Testament (Sasse).

1. The confession of sin. "If we confess our sins, He is faithful and just to forgive us our sins and to cleanse us from all unrighteousness" (1 John 1:9).

2. The confession of the content of the faith (e.g., the Creed or Small Catechism as a confession of the faith). "Since then we have a great high priest who has passed through the heavens, Jesus, the Son of God, let us hold fast our confession" (Hebrews 4:14).

3. The confession of praise. "In order that the Gentiles might glorify God for His mercy. As it is written, 'Therefore I will praise [the original has "confess"] You among the Gentiles, and sing to Your name'" (Romans 15:9).

All three are deeply connected and belong together in the life of the Christian and the Church. Without solemn confession of sin, there is no confession of the forgiveness of the Gospel. Without confession of the Gospel, there can be no joyous life of praise.

Here in the Small Catechism, we are dealing with the confession of sin and its absolution. There are several types of absolution supported by the Bible, and Lutherans believe in them all. There is the public preaching of forgiveness by the pastor. There is absolution spoken by the fellow Christian in brotherly conversation. There is absolution spoken in the process of examination before one receives the Lord's Supper. This is to be a part of what we today call confirmation. There is absolution after the common public confession of sin of the congregation (see Peters, *Confession and Christian Life*, 28). The Office of the Keys encompasses all of these, and all are heartily recommended and encouraged by Luther.

The Bible mandates confession of all sins before God. "But the tax collector, standing far off, would not even lift up his eyes to heaven, but beat his breast, saying, 'God, be merciful to me, a sinner!'" (Luke 18:13). The Bible mandates confession of sins before others, particularly those whom we've sinned against. "If you are offering your gift at the altar and there remember that your brother has something against you, leave your gift there before the altar and go. First be reconciled to your brother, and then come and offer your gift" (Matthew 5:23–24). The Bible does not mandate confession before a pastor, but gives us examples of such confession. "David said to Nathan [the prophet], 'I have sinned against the Lord.' And Nathan said to David, 'The Lord also has put away your sin; you shall not die'" (2 Samuel 12:13). The Lutheran Church requires at least once that a person be "examined and absolved" before one begins to commune. "No one is admitted to the Sacrament without first being examined" (AC XXIV 6). Private confession before a pastor is a matter of freedom, but highly recommended. "Our people are taught that they should highly prize the Absolution as being God's voice and pronounced by God's command" (AC XXV 3). In the Augsburg Confession, Lutherans admit that private "Confession is of human right only. Nevertheless, because of the great benefit of Absolution, and because it is otherwise useful to the conscience, Confession is retained among us" (AC XXV 12–13).

This part of the catechism comes purposely between Baptism and the Lord's Supper. It elaborates on daily living one's baptismal life, confessing sins before God and before others, and most important, receiving the Absolution. We come before God confessing our sins with a "joyful trembling" (Luther, in Peters, *Confession and Christian Life*, 21), confident of the Absolution spoken by God Himself on human lips. The Ten Commandments are my constant reminder, my constant accuser. They are the mirror in which I stare face-to-face with a sinner, no make-up, no veil, no complimentary lighting. I see a sinner, warts and all. The Gospel (Creed, Second and Third Articles) and Baptism are my remedy. Confession is my way of life as a baptized, honest child of God, prepared for the very body and blood of Jesus in the Supper.

The Small Catechism instructs us particularly about the blessing of confession of sins before our pastor, or private Confession and Absolution. Prior to the Lutheran Reformation, the emphasis in such confession was on the confessor listing all sins and commencing the performance of works to merit forgiveness. "The medieval auricular confession and absolution brought front and center the repentant action [works] of the penitent as a sin-cancelling human work before God" (Peters, *Confession and Christian Life*, 11). This led to troubled consciences and doubt. The biblical emphasis of the Lutherans was on the absolution and the promises of God in Christ. Such absolution gives a sinner a clear conscience, confidence, and joy.

Confession has two parts. First, that we confess our sins,

Below an example of such confession is provided. *Lutheran Service Book* provides an appropriate order. Confession cannot be overemphasized. I cannot be a Christian without the confession of my sin. Sin unconfessed withers a Christian's heart. Sin rules where it is not confessed and killed. If sin can rule a saint like David or St. Peter, or even a Judas, who spent years with Jesus, what can it do to me, worm that I am? Sin unconfessed between spouses sours marriages, often irretrievably. Sin unconfessed to children teaches them that the business of Christianity is not to be brought home from church and is in fact meaningless for life. Sin unconfessed to parents drives a wedge that may not be overcome for decades. Sins confessed before my pastor and confessor, absolved, and followed by encouragement from Scripture open my heart and eyes to others to ask forgiveness, to be forgiven, and to live freely and Joy:fully.

. . . and second, that we receive absolution, that is, forgiveness,

"If you forgive the sins of any, they are forgiven them" (John 20:23). Jesus mandates it. He gives the blessed act of forgiving to the whole church (Matthew 18) and its pastors. As a confessing sinner, as one who has acted and does act as a confessor, I know without a shadow of a doubt that private Confession and Absolution is a powerful and healthy practice. A competent pastor will invite Confession and Absolution in all cases of pastoral care and counseling. It is profoundly freeing and healing to state the ugly facts, confess them to God, and be absolved in a way that applies the salve of the forgiving Gospel directly to the bleeding and wounded conscience. Nothing is so profoundly healthy for a challenged marriage (and which isn't from time to time?) than for spouses to follow the pastor to the front pew of the church—in the presence of the font, altar, and pulpit, where God's gifts are delivered—speak the brief order of confession, specifically and mutually admit and confess sins before a spouse, and be absolved together. There is strength for a new beginning.

. . . from the pastor as from God Himself,

The fanatic in each of us sees no essential need for hearing the Gospel preached, having Baptism performed, or receiving the Sacrament of the Altar as the very feast of life and forgiveness. The fanatic in me turns me away from the service of my pastor. He's a sinner. They all are. Paul was too (Romans 7). But he's God's man, despite himself, yoked to serve Christ and His people (that's why he wears the stole), and he's there for my good, to give me the Gospel (Luke 10:16). He's been called by God Himself through my congregation. As part of his installation as pastor, the most sacred moment of his life next to his ordination, he's been bound "never to divulge the sins confessed to [him]" (*LSB: Agenda*, Services of Ordination and Installation). Never means never. If he does so, he is subject to removal. He is there for me. "Obey your leaders and submit to them, for they are keeping watch over your souls, as those who will have to give an account. Let them do this with joy and not with groaning, for that would be of no advantage to you" (Hebrews 13:17).

. . . not doubting, but firmly believing that by it our sins are forgiven before God in heaven.

Trust the words of Jesus: "If you forgive the sins of any, they are forgiven them" (John 20:23).

What sins should we confess? **Before God we should plead guilty of all sins,**

Don't bother with excuses. Don't obfuscate. Don't lie. Don't blame others. Don't indict your spouse. Don't dwell on the sins of your children or others who have driven you into anger, hatred, jealousy, spite, unkind words, unchaste living, drunkenness, slander, gossip, and more. No matter how you've been sinned against, there is always something to confess. Be like John the Baptizer. "He confessed, and did not deny, but confessed, 'I am not the Christ'" (John 1:20). Only consider the Fifth Petition, "And forgive us our trespasses as we forgive those who trespass against us." You will have enough to confess just in your failures to forgive others. You can be the leaven for healing, but only by honestly confessing.

. . . even those we are not aware of, as we do in the Lord's Prayer;

"Who can discern his errors? Declare me innocent from hidden faults" (Psalm 19:12). Conflict makes us crazy. We allege every sin under the sun and attribute them all to the person with whom we are in conflict. We ignore Jesus' words, "[You] go" (Matthew 18:15). "So-and-so sinned against me! She'll have to come groveling at *my* feet!" Beware. "Sin is crouching at the door" (Genesis 4:7). Beware. In your self-righteousness, you are in danger of losing Christ. Beware, you Pharisee! "And He said to them, 'You are those who justify yourselves before men, but God knows your hearts. For what is exalted among men is an abomination in the sight of God'" (Luke 16:15).

. . . but before the pastor we should confess only those sins which we know and feel in our hearts.

Lord, I am guilty of all manner of sins. "Who can say, 'I have made my heart pure; I am clean from my sin'?" (Proverbs 20:9). Even when I have not committed gross outward sins, my heart and mind seethe with filth. Open the lockbox of my heart, that very place I refuse to open to You. It is crammed with idols, my precious false gods. My gods are lust, anger, revenge, hatred, envy, pride. Bring the day of the LORD to my innermost heart. "And on that day, declares the LORD of hosts, I will cut off the names of the idols from the land, so that they shall be remembered no more" (Zechariah 13:2).

Which are these? Consider your place in life according to the Ten Commandments:

The doctrine of vocation is very comforting and useful. All Christians are called. "To all those in Rome who are loved by God and called to be saints: Grace to you and peace from God our Father and the Lord Jesus Christ" (Romans 1:7). Some are called to be "apostles, teachers, pastors, and evangelists" (Ephesians 4:11). The biblical teaching of vocation also recognizes stations in life in which we find ourselves, realms in which we occupy a God-pleasing position or status. The Christian calling affects our lives in these relationships. "So, brothers, in whatever condition each was called, there let him remain with God" (1 Corinthians 7:24). Jesus Himself did not call every individual to leave house and home and parents and community to follow Him.

The Gerasene was called by Jesus to stay home and tell others of Him. "As He [Jesus] was getting into the boat, the man who had been possessed with demons begged Him that he might be with Him. And He did not permit him but said to him, 'Go home to your friends and tell them how much the Lord has done for you, and how He has had mercy on you'" (Mark 5:18–19). Christians are to use their stations in life to serve those who are right in front of them in house and home, church and community. This is God-pleasing service. By telling the story of the Good Samaritan, Jesus made the point that my "neighbor" is the person in need right under my nose (Luke 10:25–37). So the catechism lists common vocations in which we are to consider our roles in life, and it is precisely in and against these vocations that we sin.

Are you a father,

A father is to love his children. He is to protect and provide for them. He is to be a hard worker and honorable at work. He is to raise them in the "discipline and instruction of the Lord" (Ephesians 6:4). The father is to be the spiritual head of the house. He has the responsibility to see that all attend church, are Christians, and live honorably in his house. He is to be a man of the Bible. He is to be spiritual. He is to be merciful (Colossians 3:21). He is to set limits for behavior and encourage what is good and upright. He is to be the first to confess Christ and the first to confess his sins and ask forgiveness. No father is up to this task. There are sins aplenty to confess.

. . . mother,

Mothers are to care for their families, provide for the needs of the family, show compassion on the children, make sure the home is in order, and confer with the father about the physical and spiritual well-being of the family. She is to have diligence in matters of economics. She is to demonstrate a tender and loving heart after Jesus, her Savior. She should know the Scriptures and the catechism and encourage all in the house to do the same.

. . . son, daughter,

Children are to honor their parents, love them, respect them, and seek their guidance. They are to grow in knowledge of Scripture and forgive parents and siblings readily. They are to be chaste and treat others with respect. Sons are to learn about their future responsibility as loving heads of households, and daughters are to learn the Christian meaning of responsive submission, as outlined in Ephesians 5:22–33.

. . . husband,

A husband is to love his wife as Christ loved the Church, humbling himself and sacrificing his own desires for the well-being of his wife. He is to be sexually chaste and honorable, honoring his wife's high office. He should bear up under crosses and encourage his wife in all things. He should never be harsh and never speak in a demeaning or demanding way. He should lead his wife by confessing his sins to her, being forgiven by her, and thereby inviting her to confess and be absolved by him (Ephesians 5:25).

. . . wife,

A wife is to love her husband and submit to him as the Church submits to Christ, particularly as He leads the family in its spiritual life. If her husband is falling short, she is to gently and kindly, and if need be, directly and strongly encourage him to do what is right and good. She should seek a healthy and happy home life, a refuge from the world for her husband and family (Titus 2:5).

. . . or worker?

A worker is to give an honest day's labor for an honest day's pay. He or she should not slander or cause dissension or turmoil at work. A worker should put the best construction on the motive and actions of those for whom he or she works. A worker should seek advancement only by honest means, be concerned with the well-being of those for whom he or she works, and know that the Lord blesses those who are honest, hardworking, and faithful (1 Peter 2:16).

Have you been disobedient, unfaithful, or lazy?

We fail in our vocations, that is, in the relationships into which God has called and placed us.

Have you been hot-tempered, rude, or quarrelsome?

Situations constantly arise in family, home, community, and church—whether we have caused them or not—that stir up our sinful nature and cause us to sin grievously. Where we ought to give the matter a night's rest (things always look differently in the morning), hold our tongue, or talk privately with others involved toward a God-pleasing solution, we instead lose control of our emotions and tongue while we accuse and deny. This is not the action of a Christian.

Have you hurt someone by your words or deeds?

Harmful words and deeds have consequences. We have the responsibility as Christians to guard ourselves from such behavior. And when we do sin against others, we are to have the humility to receive their admonition, apologize, and ask forgiveness.

Have you stolen, been negligent, wasted anything, or done any harm?

We should not be surprised when we fall into sin. "Surely there is not a righteous man on earth who does good and never sins" (Ecclesiastes 7:20). In this life, I am far, far from perfect. I will sin, especially against those whom I love the most and live with at home, work, community, or church.

A SHORT FORM OF CONFESSION

[Luther intended the following form to serve only as an example of private confession for Christians of his time. For a contemporary form of individual confession, see *Lutheran Service Book*, pp. 292–93.]

The penitent says:

Dear confessor, I ask you please to hear my confession and to pronounce forgiveness in order to fulfill God's will.

I, a poor sinner, plead guilty before God of all sins. In particular I confess before you that as a servant, maid, etc., I, sad to say, serve my master unfaithfully, for in this and that I have not done what I was told to do. I have made him angry and caused him to curse. I have been negligent and allowed damage to be done. I have also been offensive in words and deeds. I have quarreled with my peers. I have grumbled about the lady of the house and cursed her. I am sorry for all of this and I ask for grace. I want to do better.

A master or lady of the house may say:

In particular I confess before you that I have not faithfully guided my children, servants, and wife to the glory of God. I have cursed. I have set a bad example by indecent words and deeds. I have hurt my neighbor and spoken evil of him. I have overcharged, sold inferior merchandise, and given less than was paid for.

[Let the penitent confess whatever else he has done against God's commandments and his own position.]

If, however, someone does not find himself burdened with these or greater sins, he should not trouble himself or search for or invent other sins, and thereby make confession a torture. Instead, he should mention one or two that he knows: In particular I confess that I have cursed; I have used improper words; I have neglected this or that, etc. Let that be enough.

But if you know of none at all (which hardly seems possible), then mention none in particular, but receive the forgiveness upon the general confession which you make to God before the confessor.

Then the confessor shall say:

God be merciful to you and strengthen your faith. Amen.

Furthermore:

Do you believe that my forgiveness is God's forgiveness?

Yes, dear confessor.

Then let him say:

Let it be done for you as you believe. And I, by the command of our Lord Jesus Christ, forgive you your sins in the name of the Father and of the Son and of the Holy Spirit. Amen. Go in peace.

A confessor will know additional passages with which to comfort and to strengthen the faith of those who have great burdens of conscience or are sorrowful and distressed.

This is intended only as a general form of confession.

Why am I Joy:fully Lutheran?

Because I have the gift of a pastor who is called to serve me in the name of Christ and with Christ's own Word of Law and Gospel in Confession and Absolution.

You **instruct** me, Lord, that You are pleased to have Your pastors speak Your word of Absolution into my very ears. Confession and Absolution is the pattern of a daily Christian life.

I **thank** You, Lord, that You abundantly provide means for Your forgiveness and especially that when my sins trouble me, when crosses bear on me, when the sins of others perplex me and cause me to sin, I may confess these before my pastor and be absolved according to Your Word.

I **confess** that I have made all too little use of private Confession and Absolution. I have thought of asking to see my pastor, but I have been thwarted by pride, shame, and embarrassment.

Forgive me my sins. Cause me to treasure Your Gospel, and equip my pastor and all pastors to care for souls that I and as many as are in need take advantage of this blessing.

CHAPTER 29

THE OFFICE OF THE KEYS
What is the Office of the Keys?*

The Office of the Keys is that special authority which Christ has given to His church on earth to forgive the sins of repentant sinners, but to withhold forgiveness from the unrepentant as long as they do not repent.

Where is this written?*

This is what St. John the Evangelist writes in chapter twenty: The Lord Jesus breathed on His disciples and said, "Receive the Holy Spirit. If you forgive anyone his sins, they are forgiven; if you do not forgive them, they are not forgiven." (John 20:22–23)

What do you believe according to these words?*

I believe that when the called ministers of Christ deal with us by His divine command, in particular when they exclude openly unrepentant sinners from the Christian congregation and absolve those who repent of their sins and want to do better, this is just as valid and certain, even in heaven, as if Christ our dear Lord dealt with us Himself.

*This question may not have been composed by Luther himself but reflects his teaching and was included in editions of the catechism during his lifetime.

Let me hear joy and gladness; let the bones that
You have broken rejoice. **(PSALM 51:8)**

***What is the Office of the Keys?* The Office of the Keys is that special authority which Christ has given to His church on earth to forgive the sins of repentant sinners,**

It's called the Office of the "Keys" because of what Jesus said to Peter in Matthew 16:19: "I will give you the keys of the kingdom of heaven, and whatever you bind on earth shall be bound in heaven, and whatever you loose on earth shall be loosed in heaven." Jesus' words here address Peter ("you" is singular), but does this mean only Peter had the "keys"? Does the act of Confession and Absolution ultimately flow from and remain under the authority of Peter? Mind you, it's a long way still to get to a pope as "Peter." John 20:23 adds another clue.

> On the evening of that day, the first day of the week, the doors being locked where the disciples were for fear of the Jews, Jesus came and stood among them and said to them, "Peace be with you." When He had said this, He showed them His hands and His side. Then the disciples were glad when they saw the Lord. Jesus said to them again, "Peace be with you. As the Father has sent Me, even so I am sending you." And when He had said this, He breathed on them and said to them, "Receive the Holy Spirit. If you forgive the sins of any, they are forgiven them; if you withhold forgiveness from any, it is withheld." (John 20:19–23)

Note here that Jesus speaks to "them"—"the disciples." So, the Keys are not given solely to Peter by Jesus, but to "the disciples." Does this mean that only those who were witnesses of the resurrection obtained the Keys from Jesus? Or are the Keys given here only to the apostles as the first pastors? Note Matthew 18.

> If your brother sins against you, go and tell him his fault, between you and him alone. If he listens to you, you have gained your brother. But if he does not listen, take one or two others along with you, that every charge may

be established by the evidence of two or three witnesses. If he refuses to listen to them, tell it to the church. And if he refuses to listen even to the church, let him be to you as a Gentile and a tax collector. Truly, I say to you, whatever you bind on earth shall be bound in heaven, and whatever you loose on earth shall be loosed in heaven. Again I say to you, if two of you agree on earth about anything they ask, it will be done for them by My Father in heaven. For where two or three are gathered in My name, there am I among them. (Matthew 18:15–20)

Here the individual Christian is first to go and reconcile. Luther understands that each Christian is to offer the absolution in his or her vocational life. For this passage is directed "to every Christian and to each member individually" (WA 2:723.2; see Peters, *Confession and Christian Life*, 77, for many such references). If the first step fails, one is to tell it to the church precisely as Jesus directs: "tell it to the church" (Matthew 18:17). "The Keys have been given to the Church, and not merely to certain persons" (Tr 68). The Church has the Keys because every one of the baptized is given the Keys in his or her Baptism. The words of 1 Peter 2:9 "apply to the True Church" (Tr 69). The Keys are exercised publicly, in the name of Christ and the Church, by called pastors. Who has the Keys? Every baptized Christian. Every called pastor. The Church.

. . . but to withhold forgiveness from the unrepentant as long as they do not repent.

"You don't speak for God, Pastor!" "You don't speak for God, congregation!" Well, yes, they do, if they are speaking truth and calling an unrepentant sinner to repent, according to God's Word. In fact, the pastor who can't speak the Law surely can hardly speak the Gospel. And the church that cannot curse open, unrepentant sin cannot bless either. St. Paul demonstrates that in Galatians where he does both. Paul also warns how dangerous it is for those who confront an unrepentant sinner. "Brothers, if anyone is caught in any transgression, you who are spiritual should restore him in a spirit of gentleness. Keep watch on yourself, lest you too be tempted" (Galatians 6:1).

Where is this written?

If it's not in the Bible, forget it. The authority of the Church goes not one whit beyond the Bible, but neither is it one whit less than the clear Word of God (1 Corinthians 4:6)!

This is what St. John the Evangelist writes in chapter twenty: The Lord Jesus breathed on His disciples and said, "Receive the Holy Spirit. If you forgive anyone his sins, they are forgiven; if you do not forgive them, they are not forgiven." (John 20:22–23)

Here the gift of the Spirit, given before Pentecost, is given to the disciples, probably to the apostles as the first to serve in the apostolic Office of the Ministry. But as Hermann Sasse noted about Matthew 28, the argument about who got the mandate to baptize and teach is moot, because at that moment those present were the sum total of the apostles and the church.

What do you believe according to these words? **I believe that when the called ministers of Christ**

I'd better listen to my Christian brother or sister who comes to me and kindly points out my sin. If the church comes to me through its called pastor, I had *really* better listen. If some uncalled flake who knows neither Confession and Absolution nor the Office of the Keys and does not represent the true Church comes to me and tries to accuse me of some pseudosin, I'll tip my hat and say, "No thanks."

. . . deal with us by His divine command,

Jesus' words themselves are His "divine command." God deals with us through His chosen means, not ours. Here Christ tells me explicitly how the church is to deal with me if I am openly sinful and unrepentant. The rules of evidence apply in the church. Action may not be taken on the basis of mere gossip or hearsay. Truth must be established and by witnesses (1 Timothy 5:19).

. . . in particular when they exclude openly unrepentant sinners from the Christian congregation

This means the specific privileges of membership in the Christian congregation: participation in the Lord's Supper, serving as sponsors at Baptism, Christian burial. Those who have been told to refrain from the Lord's Supper until there is repentance and the fruit thereof, and even those removed from membership, are welcomed and encouraged to hear the Word preached and attend church (though this rarely happens).

. . . and absolve those who repent of their sins and want to do better,

This is the goal. We are all sinners. Admit your sin and join us repentant sinners on our knees. How much worse do we make such situations when members of the congregation are unloving, gossipy, uncharitable, and the like? Hypocrisy is a horrid sin. Jesus directed most of His preaching of the Law at "upstanding churchgoers"—the Pharisees (Matthew 23:13)!

. . . this is just as valid and certain, even in heaven, as if Christ our dear Lord dealt with us Himself.

This is what the Bible teaches about the Keys. "Truly, I say to you, whatever you bind on earth shall be bound in heaven, and whatever you loose on earth shall be loosed in heaven" (Matthew 18:18).

It's an awesome and humbling responsibility. In fact, pastors and elders who have had to carry the binding Key, knowing full well their own sin, know it's a sad and terrible responsibility. But the Law is administered for good. Through the Law comes repentance and the loosing Key! Thanks be to God! "For His anger is but for a moment, and His favor is for a lifetime. Weeping may tarry for the night, but joy comes with the morning" (Psalm

30:5). "Just so, I tell you, there will be more joy in heaven over one sinner who repents than over ninety-nine righteous persons who need no repentance" (Luke 15:7).

Why am I Joy:fully Lutheran?

Because not only has Christ won forgiveness and redemption for us on the cross, but He also gives His Church His own awesome and humbling authority and His own prescription for administering it for the eternal blessing of us sinners.

Merciful Lord, You **instruct** us precisely how we are to deal with sin and failings in the church; You provide the pastoral office to deal publicly for the benefit of those who fall into public sin.

Patient Savior, I **thank** You that time and again in the midst of human failing and sins Your Church, according to Your own command, exercises the Office of the Keys.

Gracious Savior, I **confess** my own failure to deal with sin as You direct. I **confess** my own hardness of heart when others have pointed out sins in my life. I **confess** there have been times when I have failed to have the courage and faith to be Your ambassador of Law and Gospel.

Lord of forgiveness, I pray You grant Your Church steadfast adherence to Your Word. Grant me and all Christians constant repentance and humility. Open my ears when they are closed against a brother bearing Your Word on Your mission to me. Grant repentance and faith to all who fall. Amen.

THE SACRAMENT
OF THE ALTAR

As the head of the family should teach it
in a simple way to his household

CHAPTER 30

The Sacrament of the Altar –Part One

What is the Sacrament of the Altar?

> It is the true body and blood of our Lord Jesus Christ under the bread and wine, instituted by Christ Himself for us Christians to eat and to drink.

Where is this written?

> The holy Evangelists Matthew, Mark, Luke, and St. Paul write:
>
> Our Lord Jesus Christ, on the night when He was betrayed, took bread, and when He had given thanks, He broke it and gave it to the disciples and said: "Take, eat; this is My body, which is given for you. This do in remembrance of Me."
>
> In the same way also He took the cup after supper, and when He had given thanks, He gave it to them, saying, "Drink of it, all of you; this cup is the new testament in My blood, which is shed for you for the forgiveness of sins. This do, as often as you drink it, in remembrance of Me."

For You make him most blessed forever; You make him glad with the joy of Your presence. **(PSALM 21:6)**

Dear Lord Jesus, You offer me in Your Supper the greatest mystery—Your very body and blood for the forgiveness of all my sins. In Your flesh, "the whole fullness of the deity dwells bodily" (Colossians 2:9). If I believe the words of this, Your solemn last will and testament, it is a mystery at which I tremble.

To receive the blessings of Christ's gift of His body and blood, Christians must know the basic answer to a few simple but very significant questions posed by the catechism, but "established through the words by which Christ has instituted this Sacrament" (LC V1). They are questions that require no superior intellectual ability. In Wittenberg, Luther communed children as young as seven or eight years old who could faithfully answer these simple questions. "What is it? What are its benefits? and Who is to receive it?" (LC V 1). "For it is not our intention to let people come to the Sacrament and administer it to them if they do not know what they seek or why they come" (LC V 2). Thus closed Communion. "For anyone who eats and drinks without discerning the body eats and drinks judgment on himself" (1 Corinthians 11:29).

What is the Sacrament of the Altar? It is the true body and blood of our Lord Jesus Christ

"This (bread) is My body." "This cup (wine) is My blood." Jesus, God Incarnate, says this is so. The words are unbelievably simple. The greatest minds in history spent lifetimes contemplating these words. In keeping with His way of giving us His greatest blessings through mundane things or persons (water in Baptism, spoken word, a pastor, a brother or sister in Christ, sinners who are the Church), Jesus gives us Himself, His divine body and blood, via the humblest and most common elements of bread and wine. Bread is a basic staple that sustains physical life. Wine is a gift that brings joy and conviviality to human discourse, family, and association.

> You cause the grass to grow for the livestock
> > and plants for man to cultivate,
> that he may bring forth food from the earth
> > and wine to gladden the heart of man,
> oil to make his face shine
> > and bread to strengthen man's heart. (Psalm 104:14–15)

In His Supper, Christ makes nothing less than His own body and blood—the very body and blood that hung on a cross and was raised from the dead—available to set a feast for His own. His words make it so. For "as soon as Christ says: 'This is My body," His body is there because of the Word and Power of the Holy Spirit" (WA 26:282–83). "The elements of bread and wine should be consecrated or blessed for this holy use, so that Christ's body and blood may be administered. . . . This indeed happens in no other way than through the repetition and recitation of the words of institution" (FC SD VII 82).

. . . under the bread and wine,

There is a sacramental union of Christ's own body and blood with bread and wine in the Supper; in some ways, though not all, this union is like His own incarnation, when "the Word became flesh and dwelt among us" (John 1:14). Just as Christ appeared like any other man and suffered all the infirmities and blessings and joys of any man, "yet without sin" (Hebrews 4:15), so bread and wine appear and taste like mere bread and wine. In fact, bread and wine remain bread and wine. But as St. Paul's divine and inerrant commentary of the Supper says, "The cup of blessing that we bless, is it not a participation in the blood of Christ? The bread that we break, is it not a participation in the body of Christ?" (1 Corinthians 10:16). If I receive the Supper flippantly, not believing Christ's true body and blood are present in the bread and wine, I sin against the body and blood present. "Whoever, therefore, eats the bread or drinks the cup of the Lord in an unworthy manner will be guilty concerning the body and blood of the Lord" (1 Corinthians 11:27). This is serious. "For anyone who eats and drinks without discerning the body eats and drinks judgment on himself" (1 Corinthians 11:29).

Thus pastors ("servants of Christ and stewards of the mysteries of God" [1 Corinthians 4:1], who "will have to give an account" [Hebrews 13:17]) and congregations have an awesome responsibility. "For it is not our intention to let people come to the Sacrament and administer it to them if they do not know what they seek or why they come" (LC V 2). If the Sacrament were our work, if it were a symbol of Christ who is absent, if it were our meal to show our diligence or how we love others, there would be no need for such care by pastors, congregations, and individual Christians.

. . . instituted by Christ Himself

The Lord Himself says, "This is the one to whom I will look: he who is humble and contrite in spirit and trembles at My word" (Isaiah 66:2). Christ's Word cannot be omitted. Christ's words in the Sacrament may not be changed. Christ's Word cannot be taken lightly. Christ's Word cannot be interpreted away. Christ's words stand for all time.

. . . for us Christians to eat and to drink.

The Sacrament is for Christians. Christians believe the Gospel. Christians recognize the Sacrament as Jesus' own solemn gift to the Church. Christians are repentant. Christians do not reject the Word of God in whole or in part, much less these Words of Institution. Christians confess Christ when they receive the Sacrament. "For as often as you eat this bread and drink the cup, you proclaim the Lord's death until He comes" (1 Corinthians 11:26). Christians eat and drink the body and blood. Christ's mandate is to eat and drink. Doing anything else with the elements is outside Christ's express command. This is why it is the best practice to treat the elements reverently during and after distribution. With small effort, it is possible to consecrate very nearly what is needed for a celebration of the Supper and for the pastors and elders to consume what remains, which was the practice of Dr. Luther, Dr. Walther, and our forefathers who so treasured the Sacrament and Christ's own words, "eat" and "drink."

Where is this written? The holy Evangelists Matthew, Mark, Luke, and St. Paul write:

The Lord's Supper is very important. It has the express mandate of Jesus Himself, given not once but four times in Holy Scripture. St. Paul's delivery of the Lord's Supper in 1 Corinthians (perhaps the earliest written account of the four; ca. AD 55) demonstrates that the Supper was in full use before he became a Christian (ca. AD 36). "For I received from the Lord what I also delivered to you, that the Lord Jesus on the night when He was betrayed took bread" (1 Corinthians 11:23). This particular "tradition" (handing on) in the Bible is divine and mandated for the Church.

Our Lord Jesus Christ,

The God-man, Christ, knows exactly what His Church needs. The Passover lamb sacrificed on the first and succeeding Passover celebrations of the Hebrews was sacrificed for the forgiveness of sins. Its blood was placed on the lintel of the doors of each Hebrew family. The blood was smeared in the center above the doors and on each side. The blood from the center dripped to the floor. This prefigured the wounds of Christ. "Then they shall take some of the blood and put it on the two doorposts and the lintel of the houses in which they eat it. They shall eat the flesh that night, roasted on the fire; with unleavened bread and bitter herbs they shall eat it" (Exodus 12:7–8). Christ is our great Passover Lamb! "For Christ, our Passover lamb, has been sacrificed" (1 Corinthians 5:7). "But when Christ had offered for all time a single sacrifice for sins, He sat down at the right hand of God" (Hebrews 10:12).

. . . on the night when He was betrayed,

Christ knew what was coming. "'I, when I am lifted up from the earth, will draw all people to Myself.' He said this to show by what kind of death He was going to die" (John 12:32–33). That's why He was in Gethsemane praying before He was betrayed by Judas. It was earlier that very night when He celebrated the Passover feast (how appropriate that the great and final Lamb of God was slain on Passover to end all Passovers). That very night, when He was speaking very forthrightly with His disciples after the Passover meal, He instituted His Supper.

. . . took bread, and when He had given thanks,

Jesus never omits thanksgiving when He distributes bread. "He took the seven loaves and the fish, and having given thanks He broke them and gave them to the disciples, and the disciples gave them to the crowds" (Matthew 15:36). Hearts of faith respond to gifts with thanksgiving, acknowledging their Giver. "And let them offer sacrifices of thanksgiving, and tell of His deeds in songs of joy!" (Psalm 107:22). If I shall be joyous in this life, if I shall recognize all my blessings in spouse, children, all I have, but especially my blessings in the mighty deeds of God in my Baptism, Absolution, and the Lord's Supper, and even like Jesus—in the very depths of trial and temptation—I shall respond in faith to God in thanksgiving, or I shall live faithlessly.

. . . He broke it and gave it to the disciples

This is what happened to the unleavened loaf as He separated it in order to distribute it. He did not break it to symbolize His soon to be broken body. In fact, the Gospel tells us specifically (John 19:36).

. . . and said: "Take, eat; this is My body, which is given for you.

He could have spoken it no more plainly. It is His last will and (new) testament. Men don't use picture language when writing a will. That would be endless confusion. "This bread, which I hold in my hands, is My body." He could well have said, "This bread is a sign of my body." He could well have taken the Passover lamb and said, "Now this lamb will forever signify Me as often as you eat it." But He did not. "With the bread and wine the body and blood of Christ are truly and essentially present, offered, and received" (FC SD VII 14). After the consecration, body and blood are present. They are offered by the hands of the pastor and received by the mouth of the communicant. They are there not in a butcher shop kind of way. They are there in a supernatural way. The mouth receives body and blood no matter what the heart believes. Faith does not put Jesus in the Sacrament. Jesus puts Jesus in the Sacrament by His words.

. . . This do in remembrance of Me."

Jesus says this is to be done. Hardly an hour has passed since that second day of April, AD 33, when Christ's Supper has not been celebrated. "Remembrance" hardly means "absence." "Behold, I am with you always, to the end of the age" (Matthew 28:20). When I sit with my sons and recall with joy blessings we've experienced at the hand of God, I am remembering such blessings with those sons in their presence. Christ, since His ascension, fills the universe (see Ephesians 1:23), is present where and as He wills, and is specifically with His body and blood in this Sacrament. To remember is to "proclaim the Lord's death until He comes" (1 Corinthians 11:26). As such, the Words of Institution are missionary. They are the Gospel. They proclaim the Gospel even when, for whatever reason, a person does not receive the body and blood.

In the same way also He took the cup after supper,

The cup follows. It's Christ's mandate that those who commune receive both host and cup.

. . . and when He had given thanks,

Again, thanksgiving never fails to acknowledge the mighty deeds of the Lord.

. . . He gave it to them, saying, "Drink of it, all of you;

The cup (wine) is "a participation in the blood of Christ" (1 Corinthians 10:16) and nothing less.

. . . this cup is the new testament in My blood,

And the cup is a "new testament." Things changed with Jesus. The Old Testament was a testament of forgiveness by the blood of animals. "For it is impossible for the blood of bulls and goats to take away sins" (Hebrews 10:4). That is, the sacrifices had to be repeated over and again. Christ died once for all. "He does away with the first [covenant] in order to establish the second. And by that will we have been sanctified through the offering of the body of Jesus Christ once for all" (Hebrews 10:9–10). The benefits of this once-for-all sacrifice are distributed in the cup.

. . . which is shed for you for the forgiveness of sins.

"The blood of Jesus His Son cleanses us from all sin" (1 John 1:7), first shed on a cross, now distributed from a cup.

This do, as often as you drink it,

I can come up with what seem reasonable excuses to ignore this mandate of Jesus Himself. But He says to me directly, "If you abide in My word, you are truly My disciples, and you will know the truth, and the truth will set you free" (John 8:31–32).

. . . in remembrance of Me."

"O Lord, I have heard the report of You, and Your work, O Lord, do I fear. In the midst of the years revive it; in the midst of the years make it known; in wrath remember mercy" (Habakkuk 3:2).

Why am I Joy:fully Lutheran?

I am Joy:fully Lutheran because Christ was sacrificed once for all for my sins and the sins of the whole world. In His Supper, He—according to His exceedingly clear Word and testament—gives me His very body and blood for my good. "What Christ's lips say and speak, so it is. He can never lie or deceive" (LC V 14). Joy.

Dear Jesus, Your Word **instructs** me that on the night in which You were betrayed, You established, mandated, and empowered Your own Supper and determined that where that Supper is carried out according to Your words, You feed Christians with Your very body and blood.

Dear Jesus, I **thank** You that in the very act of giving me Your body and blood, You embedded for all time Your thanksgiving to God the Father in Your Words of Institution.

Dear Jesus, I **confess** that words fail when I consider that, worm that I am, I am invited to kneel at Your Table and receive Your body and blood in bread and wine. I **confess** words fail me when I desire to render You thanks that You—almighty God in the flesh—are pleased to descend and feed me, sinner of sinners.

Dear Jesus, cause me to love Your Supper! Cause me to seek Your body and blood often! Forgive me! Strengthen my faith! When I might cry, "Lord, depart from me, for I am a sinful man!" (Luke 5:8), strengthen me to say, "Lord, I believe in Your body and blood! Help my unbelief!" Amen.

CHAPTER 31

THE SACRAMENT OF THE ALTAR –PART TWO

What is the benefit of this eating and drinking?

> These words, "Given and shed for you for the forgiveness of sins," show us that in the Sacrament forgiveness of sins, life, and salvation are given us through these words. For where there is forgiveness of sins, there is also life and salvation.

With joy and gladness they are led along as they enter the palace of the king. **(PSALM 45:15)**

"I am the living bread that came down from heaven. If anyone eats of this bread, he will live forever. And the bread that I will give for the life of the world is My flesh" (John 6:51). St. John's incredible Gospel is packed deeply with content that never ceases to surprise and bring joy to the student of the Bible. In the Pauline Letters, the word *flesh* is used negatively to mean "sinful flesh," but in John, the word is more often used for the blessed incarnation of Jesus, the "flesh" of God in human form in Christ. It's a very strong word. Already at the time St. John wrote his Gospel, heretics were denying that Jesus actually was God who took on a real human body. We have trouble believing Jesus the man was God. In the first century, they (the Platonists, separating physical and spiritual) had trouble believing that Christ the God was really a man. John carefully composed his Gospel using the words of Jesus and, under the inspiration of the Holy Spirit, translated Jesus' Aramaic and Hebrew words into the most helpful Greek words in his Gospel.

We are informed that when the traveling tent/tabernacle was created in the days of Moses, "the cloud covered the tent of meeting, and the glory of the LORD filled the tabernacle" (Exodus 40:34). This "cloud" was the presence of Yahweh. When the tabernacle traveled, God's presence led the people as a pillar of cloud by day and a pillar of fire by night. When the tabernacle was set up, His presence filled the holy of holies, that secret chamber where once a year the high priest sprinkled the blood of a sacrificed lamb to cover the sins of the people. The Greek translation of the Old Testament Bible, which was known to and used by the apostles and especially St. Paul, translated the Hebrew word for "glory" as "doxa." So when John writes, "The Word became flesh and dwelt among us. And we have beheld His glory (*doxa*)," he is less than subtly making a statement about who Jesus is. Indeed, "the Word was with God, and the Word was God" (John 1:1)! And in fact, Yahweh's own divine glory now dwells in Jesus Christ in the flesh. John 1:14 says literally, "The Word of God became flesh and tented/tabernacled among us." Only a chapter later in John, Jesus talks of Himself as the temple (the place of the glory of the Lord since the building of Solomon's temple to replace the tabernacle). "But He was speaking about the temple of His body" (John 2:21). Not only is Jesus Yahweh in the flesh, but His flesh is the place where God's forgiving presence resides!

Thus when Jesus died "the curtain of the temple was torn in two, from top to bottom. And the earth shook, and the rocks were split" (Matthew 27:51). The New Testament era had dawned, and it was all about this God in the flesh, Jesus.

Jesus famously spoke of His flesh as bread from heaven in John 6.

> Truly, truly, I say to you, whoever believes has eternal life. I am the bread of life. Your fathers ate the manna in the wilderness, and they died. This is the bread that comes down from heaven, so that one may eat of it and not die. I am the living bread that came down from heaven. If anyone eats of this bread, he will live forever. And the bread that I will give for the life of the world is My flesh. (vv. 47–51)

The Pharisees objected, and Jesus pushed even further.

The Jews then disputed among themselves, saying, "How can this man give us His flesh to eat?" So Jesus said to them, "Truly, truly, I say to you, unless you eat the flesh of the Son of Man and drink His blood, you have no life in you. Whoever feeds on My flesh and drinks My blood has eternal life, and I will raise him up on the last day. For My flesh is true food, and My blood is true drink. Whoever feeds on My flesh and drinks My blood abides in Me, and I in him. As the living Father sent Me, and I live because of the Father, so whoever feeds on Me, he also will live because of Me. This is the bread that came down from heaven, not like the bread the fathers ate, and died. Whoever feeds on this bread will live forever." (vv. 52–58)

Was Jesus speaking of the Supper here? For various and good reasons, Luther followed St. Augustine and said no. Here "eat" is as much as "believe." Others, like Hermann Sasse and Werner Elert, say yes. Jesus begins with the metaphor of calling Himself "bread from heaven" but pushes beyond to reference the "flesh" that He would give in His Supper. And this, say Sasse and Elert, was John's way of both hiding the Sacrament (which was being ridiculed and slandered as occult practice including even the murder of children) and sticking the teaching of Christ's incarnation and body and blood in the Sacrament right in the face of the deniers. For those who denied God could be man also denied bread and wine could be body and blood.

Regardless of that debate, Jesus says His flesh is life-giving. And we know definitively from the Words of Institution that Jesus gives us His flesh, His body and blood, in the Sacrament. And we know definitively why He gives us such flesh: "For the forgiveness of sins."

These words, "Given and shed for you for the forgiveness of sins," show us that in the Sacrament forgiveness of sins,

The catechism is simple enough. And in the end, it's about a very simple theme. Law and Gospel. Sin and forgiveness. The Sacrament is about Christ for me, Christ for forgiveness. The one thing the Church cannot live without is Christ and His forgiveness. The Gospel demands faith but gives it at the same time. Otherwise it would not be the Gospel! "This faith He Himself demands in the Word when He says, 'Given . . . and shed for you,' as if He said, 'For this reason I give it, and ask you to eat and drink it, that you may claim it as yours and enjoy it'" (LC V 34).

. . . life,

The Sacrament of Christ's body and blood works life. Life is in the blood. Blood separated from the sacrifice is death for the sacrifice, but the blood atones for the life of the sinner. "For the life of the flesh is in the blood, and I have given it for you on the altar to make atonement for your souls, for it is the blood that makes atonement by the life" (Leviticus 17:11).

Christ's blood is our atoning sacrifice. Now the delivery of that blood in the Sacrament means life for those who receive it in faith.

. . . and salvation are given us through these words.

Human words can stir up memories. They can gin up courage. They can enflame temporary excitement. They can cause a great outcry and do great good or harm. But they cannot heal the lame man. They cannot raise the dead. They cannot (but by the name of Jesus) speak forgiveness valid before God.

> And when Jesus saw their faith, He said to the paralytic, "Take heart, My son; your sins are forgiven." And behold, some of the scribes said to themselves, "This man is blaspheming." But Jesus, knowing their thoughts, said, "Why do you think evil in your hearts? For which is easier, to say, 'Your sins are forgiven,' or to say, 'Rise and walk'? But that you may know that the Son of Man has authority on earth to forgive sins"—He then said to

the paralytic—"Rise, pick up your bed and go home." And he rose and went home. When the crowds saw it, they were afraid, and they glorified God, who had given such authority to men. (Matthew 9:2–8)

For where there is forgiveness of sins, there is also life and salvation.

Jesus' words do everything we need. The supper is a foretaste of the feast to come. "For I tell you that from now on I will not drink of the fruit of the vine until the kingdom of God comes" (Luke 22:18). The feast will continue in heaven and with heavenly joy. "He will wipe away every tear from their eyes, and death shall be no more, neither shall there be mourning, nor crying, nor pain anymore, for the former things have passed away" (Revelation 21:4).

***How can bodily eating and drinking do such great things?* Certainly not just eating and drinking do these things,**

The Supper is not just the eating and drinking. The Supper is not just the presence of God. The Supper is not just a bit of wine and bread. The Supper is not the Church's or the individual's action.

. . . but the words written here: "Given and shed for you for the forgiveness of sins."

The Supper is for us what the hot coal was for Isaiah.

And the foundations of the thresholds shook at the voice of him who called, and the house was filled with smoke. And I said: "Woe is me! For I am lost; for I am a man of unclean lips, and I dwell in the midst of a people of unclean lips; for my eyes have seen the King, the LORD of hosts!"

Then one of the seraphim flew to me, having in his hand a burning coal that he had taken with tongs from the altar. And he touched my mouth and said: "Behold, this has touched your lips; your guilt is taken away, and your sin atoned for." (Isaiah 6:4–7)

Touched by the burning coal of Christ's most precious body and blood, I am forgiven and in the presence of God. And thus we sing with the seraphs in His presence, "Holy is the Lord of hosts!" (Isaiah 6:3). And we will sing the same song with all the saints in eternity around the throne of the Lamb.

These words, along with the bodily eating and drinking, are the main thing in the Sacrament. Whoever believes these words has exactly what they say: "forgiveness of sins."

I believe, Lord. I believe that I may have life in Your name (John 20:31). "The words that I have spoken to you are spirit and life" (John 6:63).

WHY AM I JOY:FULLY LUTHERAN?

I believe that in the Sacrament I receive "the forgiveness of sins, life, and salvation." And to make it all the more certain, Christ says it is "for you."

Lord of the Sacrament, You promise and place in the Supper the sure promise of the forgiveness of sins. And You **instruct** me to come to the Supper when You say it is given "for you."

Lord of heaven, I **thank** You. For with the forgiveness of sins come a quiet conscience, confidence in the midst of trial and temptation, and the present promise of eternal life.

Lord of the Church, I **confess** I am all too sluggish in seeking Your Sacrament. You regard my sins as weighty as Your own death, indeed, the sacrifice of Your body and blood. You regard my sins as serious enough for You to institute Your blessed Supper. Forgive me by Your body and blood.

Lord of eternity, cause me to rejoice in the forgiveness

You give, and open my mouth and give me lips to praise Your name, especially among all those who don't know Your blessed Supper. Amen.

CHAPTER 32

The Sacrament of the Altar –Part Three

Who receives this sacrament worthily?

> Fasting and bodily preparation are certainly fine outward training. But that person is truly worthy and well prepared who has faith in these words: "Given and shed for you for the forgiveness of sins."

> But anyone who does not believe these words or doubts them is unworthy and unprepared, for the words "for you" require all hearts to believe.

Then I will go to the altar of God, to God my exceeding joy, and I will praise You with the lyre, O God, my God. **(PSALM 43:4)**

Fasting and bodily preparation are certainly fine outward training.

Lord, I am lazy. I am satiated. "The spirit indeed is willing, but the flesh is weak" (Matthew 26:41). The Large Catechism says that "fasting, prayer, and other such things" are good and "may indeed be outward preparations and discipline for children, so that the body may keep and bring itself modestly and reverently to receive Christ's body and blood" (LC V 37). I have used my freedom to ignore Your own example of fasting (Matthew 4:2). You, Lord, fasted forty days and nights. I have trouble fasting forty minutes. I have ignored Your own words, which presume fasting among the faithful: "And when you fast, do not look gloomy like the hypocrites" (Matthew 6:16). Lead me in the proper preparation for Your Sacrament, particularly in repentance and in considering of the magnitude of the gifts.

But that person is truly worthy and well prepared who has

faith in these words: "Given and shed for you for the forgiveness of sins."

I come to the table a sinner. I confess my sins in the general confession but spend too little time considering my failings for even minutes prior to the Sunday morning service. I approach Your altar. My mind wanders. I kneel. I remember my sins, my troubling sins, the sins that beset me and harass me. I am weak. I do not lift up my eyes . . . until my pastor lays the host in my open, begging hand. "Take, eat; this is the true body of our Lord and Savior Jesus Christ, given for you." I bow my head again, burdened but confident. I life my eyes to the cup. "Take, drink; this is the true blood of our Lord and Savior Jesus Christ, given and shed for you for the forgiveness of sins." I am forgiven. I am fortified. In hope and assurance, I listen again: "The body and blood of your Lord and Savior Jesus Christ strengthen and preserve you, body and soul, to life everlasting. Go in peace." I believe it.

But anyone who does not believe these words or doubts them is unworthy and unprepared,

Some should not come. God be merciful and grant repentance!

> Those who are lewd and morally loose must be told to stay away [1 Corinthians 5:9–13]. They are not prepared to receive forgiveness of sin, since they do not desire it and do not wish to be godly. But the others, who are not such callous and wicked people, and who desire to be godly, must not absent themselves. This is true even though otherwise they are feeble and full of infirmities. For St. Hilary also has said, "If anyone has not committed sin for which he can rightly be put out of the congregation and be considered no Christian, he ought not stay away from the Sacrament, lest he should deprive himself of life." No one will live so well that he will not have many daily weaknesses in flesh and blood. (LC V 58–60)

I may not be "such a callous and wicked" person, but I have struggled with doubts. Is this bread and wine what Christ says it is? The devil harasses me. I do believe, Lord! Help me! Is this Supper for me? I'm a sinner. Yes! It's precisely for sinners! I believe what the Scriptures teach about me. I hold my hand to my chest and confess, "No one is righteous. No, not one." "It is the highest art to know that our Sacrament does not depend upon our worthiness" (LC V 61). "Come to Me, all who labor and are heavy laden, and I will give you rest!" (Matthew 11:28). "If, therefore, you are heavy laden and feel your weakness, then go joyfully to this Sacrament and receive refreshment, comfort, and strength. If you wait until you are rid of such burdens, so that you might come to the Sacrament pure and worthy, you must stay away forever" (LC V 72–73). Besides my flesh and weakness, the world attacks me with its myriad distractions and lies. And the devil assaults me. "If you could see how many knives, darts, and arrows are every moment aimed at you, you would be glad to come to the Sacrament as often as possible" (LC V 82). Lord, I am weak. "Those who are mindful of their weakness desire to be rid of it and long for help. They should regard and use the Sacrament just like a precious antidote against the poison that they have in them" (LC V 70). Give me the medicine! "Those who are well have no need of a physician, but those who are sick" (Matthew 9:12).

. . . for the words "for you" require all hearts to believe.

What the Large Catechism says is true of me. "We go exactly because we are unworthy" (LC V 61). I do believe, Lord. Only give my heart what You require.

Why am I Joy:fully Lutheran?

I am Joy:fully Lutheran because the Lord invites precisely sinners to His Supper. "The Son of Man came not to be served but to serve, and to give His life as a ransom for many" (Matthew 20:28). Wonder of wonders, in the Supper, the almighty God of eternity in the flesh serves the least, the last, the unworthy, the doubting, the harassed, even me.

Jesus, You **instruct** me that I am to flee to You in the midst of all trouble.

Jesus, I **thank** You that in this very Sacrament of Your body and blood, You give me the very and only thing I need to receive the blessings—a repentant heart and faith in Your words.

Jesus, I **confess** that I struggle. I hurt. I am sore oppressed by my own guilt and bad conscience.

Jesus, be Jesus to me. Be my Savior in Your body and blood, given and shed for me. And give me joy.

DAILY
PRAYERS

How the head of the family should teach his household to
pray morning and evening

CHAPTER 33

Morning and Evening Prayers

Morning Prayer

In the morning when you get up, make the sign of the holy cross and say:

In the name of the Father and of the ✠ Son and of the Holy Spirit. Amen.

Then, kneeling or standing, repeat the Creed and the Lord's Prayer. If you choose, you may also say this little prayer:

I thank You, my heavenly Father, through Jesus Christ, Your dear Son, that You have kept me this night from all harm and danger; and I pray that You would keep me this day also from sin and every evil, that all my doings and life may please You. For into Your hands I commend myself, my body and soul, and all things. Let Your holy angel be with me, that the evil foe may have no power over me. Amen.

Then go joyfully to your work, singing a hymn, like that of the Ten Commandments, or whatever your devotion may suggest.

You make the going out of the morning and the evening to shout for joy. **(PSALM 65:8)**

In the morning when you get up,

"O LORD, in the morning You hear my voice; in the morning I prepare a sacrifice for You and watch" (Psalm 5:3).

. . . make the sign of the holy cross and say:

"Far be it from me to boast except in the cross of our Lord

Jesus Christ, by which the world has been crucified to me, and I to the world" (Galatians 6:14).

Making the sign of the cross is a very ancient Christian custom. Perhaps the earliest reference to the practice is from the Church Father Tertullian, who lived in ancient Carthage (North Africa). In AD 200, he wrote:

> At every forward step and movement, at every going in and out, when we put on our clothes and shoes, when we bathe, when we sit at table, when we light the lamps, on couch, on seat, in all the ordinary actions of daily life, we trace upon the forehead the sign [i.e., sign of the cross; later the practice changed from simply signing the forehead to the common practice of today]. (*ANF* 3:94–95)

In the next line, Tertullian notes that making the sign of the cross is not a mandate from Scripture. "If, for these and other such rules, you insist upon having positive Scripture injunction, you will find none" (*ANF* 3:95). Luther, however, maintained any practices in the church that he thought salutary and that did not contradict the Bible. So, he (and Lutherans for centuries almost without exception after him) maintained a very positive view of crucifixes and the sign of the cross. Note below that Luther, in the Large Catechism, also tells us why he maintained the *Benedicite* and *Gratias*, the very prayers he placed in the Small Catechism.

> To defy the devil, I say, we should always keep the holy name upon our lips so that he may not be able to harm us as he would like to do. For this purpose it also helps to form the habit of commending ourselves each day to God—our soul and body, spouse, children, servants, and all that we have—for his protection against every conceivable need. This is why the Benedicite, the Gratias, and other evening and morning blessings were also introduced and have continued among us. From the

same source comes the custom learned in childhood of making the sign of the cross when something dreadful or frightening is seen or heard, and saying, "Lord God, save me!" or, "Help, dear Lord Christ!" and the like. (Kolb and Wengert LC I 72–74)

In the name of the Father and of the ✠ Son and of the Holy Spirit. Amen.

Calling on God's name "is also a blessed and useful habit and very effective against the devil. He is ever around us and lies in wait to bring us into sin and shame, disaster and trouble [2 Timothy 2:26]. But he hates to hear God's name and cannot remain long where it is spoken and called upon from the heart" (LC I 71). This name was put on me in my Baptism, and making the sign of the cross and reciting God's name is shorthand, as it were, for remembering and confessing all the blessings of Baptism!

Then, kneeling or standing, repeat the Creed and the Lord's Prayer. If you choose, you may also say this little prayer:

Here we see something of Luther's practice as an Augustinian friar. St. Paul often knelt to pray. There is his touching departure from the Christians in Tyre on his way to Jerusalem. "When our days there were ended, we departed and went on our journey, and they all, with wives and children, accompanied us until we were outside the city. And kneeling down on the beach, we prayed" (Acts 21:5).

I thank You, my heavenly Father, through Jesus Christ, Your dear Son,

Thanksgiving to God is a *sine qua non* of joy. No thankfulness, no joy. Know thankfulness? Know joy! So Paul wrote the Thessalonians, "Rejoice always, pray without ceasing, give thanks in all circumstances; for this is the will of God in Christ Jesus for you" (1 Thessalonians 5:16–18). The power of gratitude has been demonstrated to significantly increase happiness in marriage, for instance.[4] How much stronger the force for joy when we speak thankfulness to God with His own words, as He has invited and commanded us, through Jesus Christ. "For through Him we both have access in one Spirit to the Father" (Ephesians 2:18).

. . . that You have kept me this night from all harm and danger;

How often in my prayers do I fail to thank God for the wondrous protection and preservation He provides! Thank You, Lord! Through Jesus Christ! Another night kept from physical harm!

. . . and I pray that You would keep me this day also from sin and every evil,

Lord, preserve me from my sin and the sins of others! Grant me strength of faith this day! Grant me a hunger and desire for Your Word this day! Strengthen me this day to withstand the assaults of sin, death, and the devil! It's a new day!

. . . that all my doings and life may please You.

I desire in my inmost being to please You, Lord! Lead me; direct me! Guide me by Your wholesome and life-giving Word! "You make known to me the path of life; in Your presence there is fullness of joy; at Your right hand are pleasures forevermore" (Psalm 16:11).

For into Your hands I commend myself, my body and soul, and all things.

---

4   "Research shows that merely dedicating a little time to thinking about how your partner has invested in the relationship increases positive feelings toward them and elevates commitment to the marriage. And this often leads to a virtuous cycle." Eric Barker, "How to Have a Happy Marriage: 7 Powerful Secrets from Research," August 7, 2018, https://www.bakadesuyo.com/2018/08/how-to-have-a-happy-marriage/ (accessed September 4, 2018).

Into Your hand I commit my spirit;
　　You have redeemed me, O Lord, faithful God.

I hate those who pay regard to worthless idols,
　　but I trust in the Lord.

I will rejoice and be glad in Your steadfast love,
　　because You have seen my affliction;
　　　　You have known the distress of my soul. (Psalm 31:5–7)

Let Your holy angel be with me,

The devil tried to tempt Christ with Psalm 91. But its truth stands. "For He will command His angels concerning you to guard you in all your ways" (Psalm 91:11). "The angel of the Lord encamps around those who fear Him" (Psalm 34:7).

. . . that the evil foe may have no power over me. Amen.

"Evil foe" (*der alt böse Feind*) has no precise biblical equivalent. Luther used the same description for the devil in his famous hymn "A Mighty Fortress Is Our God" ("The old evil foe, Now means deadly woe" [*LSB* 656:1]), most likely written two years before the Small Catechism. "One little word can fell him" (st. 3). That word is "Jesus." To which I say confidently, "Amen!"

Then go joyfully to your work, singing a hymn, like that of the Ten Commandments, or whatever your devotion may suggest.

The reference here is to Luther's "These Are the Holy Ten Commands" (*LSB* 581). "Let the word of Christ dwell in you richly, teaching and admonishing one another in all wisdom, singing psalms and hymns and spiritual songs, with thankfulness in your hearts to God" (Colossians 3:16).

Evening Prayer

In the evening when you go to bed, make the sign of the holy cross and say:

In the name of the Father and of the ✠ Son and of the Holy Spirit. Amen.

Then, kneeling or standing, repeat the Creed and the Lord's Prayer. If you choose, you may also say this little prayer:

I thank You, my heavenly Father, through Jesus Christ, Your dear Son, that You have graciously kept me this day; and I pray that You would forgive me all my sins where I have done wrong, and graciously keep me this night. For into Your hands I commend myself, my body and soul, and all things. Let Your holy angel be with me, that the evil foe may have no power over me. Amen.

Then go to sleep at once and in good cheer.

In peace I will both lie down and sleep; for You alone, O LORD, make me dwell in safety. **(PSALM 4:8)**

In the evening when you go to bed, make the sign of the holy cross and say:

"Looking to Jesus, the founder and perfecter of our faith, who for the joy that was set before Him endured the cross, despising the shame, and is seated at the right hand of the throne of God" (Hebrews 12:2).

In the name of the Father and of the ✠ Son and of the Holy Spirit. Amen.

"But let all who take refuge in You rejoice; let them ever sing for joy, and spread Your protection over them, that those who love Your name may exult in You" (Psalm 5:11). Oh Lord, as I make this sign of the holy cross, at the close of a day of Your blessings, whether in the form of bountiful food and goods, friends, colleagues, family, good weather, or other blessings, or even the blessings of Your crosses specifically designed for my shoulders, I confess in the face of all, including my sins, that I am Yours. Amen.

Then, kneeling or standing, repeat the Creed and the Lord's Prayer.

"May we shout for joy over Your salvation, and in the name of our God set up our banners! May the LORD fulfill all Your petitions!" (Psalm 20:5).

Martin Luther actually preferred to stand looking up and out a window as he prayed in the evening. He did so on the night he died. He spoke his prayers aloud. His friends marveled at his fervent intercessions.

Luther called the Apostles' Creed the "child's confession" [*Kinder Glaube*]. It is the (lowercase *c*) catholic staple of his firm faith in the triune God. The Lord's Prayer is his prayer staple as noted in that chief part. Luther kept the good and dumped the dross. The church, though suffering through false teachings and practices, has existed through all the centuries. The Creed and Lord's Prayer sustained the Church in faith through all the centuries. These should be my faith staples too.

The prayers Luther provides are firmly in the tradition of the Church. He no doubt spoke them virtually word-for-word every day of his monastic life. The individual phrases come largely from the Psalms. The bedtime prayer was part of the evening service of Compline (*LSB*, pp. 253–59), used by monks (Peters, *Confession and Christian Life*, 238). Luther's Evening Prayer mirrors a ninth-century prayer, though Luther's prayer removes the prayer to Mary. "Luther's . . . prayers, as has been shown, are essentially nothing other than a compilation of what had been inherited from the Latin Church" (Peters, *Confession and Christian Life*, 242). And the Latin prayers reflect strongly the very wording of a prayer of an Egyptian monk (ca. 390) from the Eastern Church, written in Greek (Peters, *Confession and Christian Life*, 242)!

If you choose, you may also say this little prayer: I thank You, my heavenly Father, through Jesus Christ, Your dear Son,

"And let them offer sacrifices of thanksgiving, and tell of His deeds in songs of joy!" (Psalm 107:22).

. . . that You have graciously kept me this day;

"Love the LORD, all you His saints! The LORD preserves the faithful but abundantly repays the one who acts in pride" (Psalm 31:23).

. . . and I pray that You would forgive me all my sins where I have done wrong.

"As for You, O LORD, You will not restrain Your mercy from me; Your steadfast love and Your faithfulness will ever preserve me!" (Psalm 40:11).

. . . and graciously keep me this night.

"My mouth will praise You with joyful lips, when I remember You upon my bed, and meditate on You in the watches of the night" (Psalm 63:5–6).

For into Your hands I commend myself, my body and soul, and all things.

"To You the helpless commits himself; You have been the helper of the fatherless" (Psalm 10:14).

Let Your holy angel be with me,

"On that day the LORD will protect the inhabitants of Jerusalem, so that the feeblest among them on that day shall be like David, and the house of David shall be like God, like the angel of the LORD, going before them" (Zechariah 12:8).

. . . that the evil foe may have no power over me. Amen.

"But the Lord is faithful. He will establish you and guard you against the evil one" (2 Thessalonians 3:3).

Then go to sleep at once and in good cheer.

"In peace I will both lie down and sleep; for You alone, O LORD, make me dwell in safety" (Psalm 4:8).

WHY AM I JOY:FULLY LUTHERAN?

Because I know that I can confidently pray in Christ's name and the name of the blessed Trinity, into which I am baptized. I know that—guided by the Small Catechism and the rich biblical witness—God delights in providing what I need and hearing and answering my prayers.

O Lord, protector of all those who look to You in faith, You richly **instruct** me to pray to You at all times, but especially at morning and evening.

I **thank** You, Lord, for the biblical wisdom of the Small Catechism and its encouragement for me to be a person of daily prayer, thanksgiving, and joy.

I **confess**, Lord, that if I pray at all, morning and evening, my prayers are rushed, are often void of Your Word, and lack right thanksgiving, joy, and concern for my body and soul and the well-being of others.

Lord, turn not away from me. I cling to Your many promises that urge us to pray and Your promise to hear and answer. Amen.

CHAPTER 34

Mealtime Prayers

How the head of the family should teach his household to ask a blessing and return thanks

Asking a Blessing

The children and members of the household shall go to the table reverently, fold their hands, and say:

The eyes of all look to You, [O Lord,] and You give them their food at the proper time. You open Your hand and satisfy the desires of every living thing. (Ps. 145:15–16)

Then shall be said the Lord's Prayer and the following:

Lord God, heavenly Father, bless us and these Your gifts which we receive from Your bountiful goodness, through Jesus Christ, our Lord. Amen.

Go, eat your bread with joy, and drink your wine with a merry heart, for God has already approved what you do. **(ECCLESIASTES 9:7)**

The children and members of the household shall go to the table reverently, fold their hands, and say:

"Train up a child in the way he should go; even when he is old he will not depart from it" (Proverbs 22:6).

The eyes of all look to You, [O Lord,] and You give them their food at the proper time. You open Your hand and satisfy the desires of every living thing. (Ps. 145:15–16)

"Listen to Me, you who pursue righteousness, you who seek the LORD: look to the rock from which you were hewn, and to the quarry from which you were dug" (Isaiah 51:1). "'And to every beast of the earth and to every bird of the heavens and to everything that creeps on the earth, everything that has the breath of life, I have given every green plant for food.' And it was so" (Genesis 1:30).

Then shall be said the Lord's Prayer and the following:
Lord God, heavenly Father, bless us and these Your gifts

"And there you shall eat before the Lord your God, and you shall rejoice, you and your households, in all that you undertake, in which the Lord your God has blessed you" (Deuteronomy 12:7).

. . . which we receive from Your bountiful goodness,

"Like newborn infants, long for the pure spiritual milk, that by it you may grow up into salvation—if indeed you have tasted that the Lord is good" (1 Peter 2:2–3).

. . . through Jesus Christ, our Lord. Amen.

"To the only God, our Savior, through Jesus Christ our Lord, be glory, majesty, dominion, and authority, before all time and now and forever. Amen" (Jude 25).

Also, after eating, they shall, in like manner, reverently and with folded hands say:

Give thanks to the LORD, for He is good. His love endures forever. [He] gives food to every creature. He provides food for the cattle and for the young ravens when they call. His pleasure is not in the strength of the horse, nor His delight in the legs of a man; the LORD delights in those who fear Him, who put their hope in His unfailing love. (Ps. 136:1, 25; 147:9–11)

Then shall be said the Lord's Prayer and the following:

We thank You, Lord God, heavenly Father, for all Your benefits, through Jesus Christ, our Lord, who lives and reigns with You and the Holy Spirit forever and ever. Amen.

Also, after eating, they shall, in like manner, reverently and with folded hands say: Give thanks to the LORD, for He is good.

"And when he [Paul] had said these things, he took bread, and giving thanks to God in the presence of all he broke it and began to eat" (Acts 27:35).

His love endures forever.

"I will rejoice and be glad in Your steadfast love, because You have seen my affliction; You have known the distress of my soul" (Psalm 31:7).

[He] gives food to every creature. He provides food for the cattle and for the young ravens when they call.

"My soul will be satisfied as with fat and rich food, and my mouth will praise You with joyful lips" (Psalm 63:5).

His pleasure is not in the strength of the horse, nor His delight in the legs of a man;

"'Scoffer' is the name of the arrogant, haughty man who acts with arrogant pride" (Proverbs 21:24).

. . . the LORD delights in those who fear Him, who put their hope in His unfailing love. (Ps. 136:1, 25; 147:9–11)

"The LORD your God is in your midst, a mighty one who will save; He will rejoice over you with gladness; He will quiet you by His love; He will exult over you with loud singing" (Zephaniah 3:17).

Why am I Joy:fully Lutheran?

The Bible is brimming with thanksgiving for all of God's blessings, including the simple daily blessings of food and drink. Knowing Christ, we are free to rejoice in these simple, daily, wonderful gifts of God.

O Lord, You **instruct** me that everything we need for this life and life eternal is a gift from You.

O Lord, I give You **thanks** for all Your abundant blessings of body and soul!

O Lord, I **confess** that I have not always prayed with due thanks at mealtimes. I have not always given the best witness to my family. In the course of the busyness of life, I often failed to create a sacred space for prayer at mealtimes.

O Lord, forgive me my many failings. Strengthen me! Instruct me! Grant me the will and ability henceforth to humbly ask Your blessing at every meal. Cover my failings and faults in Your precious and all-atoning blood. Amen.

TABLE OF DUTIES

Certain passages of Scripture for various holy orders and positions, admonishing them about their duties and responsibilities

CHAPTER 35

TABLE OF DUTIES

Not that we lord it over your faith, but we work with
you for your joy, for you stand firm in your faith.
(2 CORINTHIANS 1:24)

To Bishops, Pastors, and Preachers

The overseer must be above reproach, the husband of but
one wife, temperate, self-controlled, respectable, hospitable, able
to teach, not given to drunkenness, not violent but gentle, not
quarrelsome, not a lover of money. He must manage his own
family well and see that his children obey him with proper respect. **1 Tim. 3:2–4**

He must not be a recent convert, or he may become con-
ceited and fall under the same judgment as the devil. **1 Tim. 3:6**

He must hold firmly to the trustworthy message as it has
been taught, so that he can encourage others by sound doctrine
and refute those who oppose it. **Titus 1:9**

What the Hearers Owe Their Pastors

The Lord has commanded that those who preach the gospel
should receive their living from the gospel. **1 Cor. 9:14**

Anyone who receives instruction in the word must share all
good things with his instructor. Do not be deceived: God cannot
be mocked. A man reaps what he sows. **Gal. 6:6–7**

The elders who direct the affairs of the church well are worthy of double honor, especially those whose work is preaching
and teaching. For the Scripture says, "Do not muzzle the ox
while it is treading out the grain," and "The worker deserves his
wages." **1 Tim. 5:17–18**

We ask you, brothers, to respect those who work hard among
you, who are over you in the Lord and who admonish you. Hold
them in the highest regard in love because of their work. Live in

peace with each other. **1 Thess. 5:12–13**

Obey your leaders and submit to their authority. They keep watch over you as men who must give an account. Obey them so that their work will be a joy, not a burden, for that would be of no advantage to you. **Heb. 13:17**

Of Civil Government

Everyone must submit himself to the governing authorities, for there is no authority except that which God has established. The authorities that exist have been established by God. Consequently, he who rebels against the authority is rebelling against what God has instituted, and those who do so will bring judgment on themselves. For rulers hold no terror for those who do right, but for those who do wrong. Do you want to be free from fear of the one in authority? Then do what is right and he will commend you. For he is God's servant to do you good. But if you do wrong, be afraid, for he does not bear the sword for nothing. He is God's servant, an agent of wrath to bring punishment on the wrongdoer. **Rom. 13:1–4**

Of Citizens

Give to Caesar what is Caesar's, and to God what is God's. **Matthew 22:21**

It is necessary to submit to the authorities, not only because of possible punishment but also because of conscience. This is also why you pay taxes, for the authorities are God's servants, who give their full time to governing. Give everyone what you owe him: If you owe taxes, pay taxes; if revenue, then revenue; if respect, then respect; if honor, then honor. **Rom. 13:5–7**

I urge, then, first of all, that requests, prayers, intercession and thanksgiving be made for everyone—for kings and all those in authority, that we may live peaceful and quiet lives in all godliness and holiness. This is good, and pleases God our Savior. **1 Tim. 2:1–3**

Remind the people to be subject to rulers and authorities, to be obedient, to be ready to do whatever is good. **Titus 3:1**

Submit yourselves for the Lord's sake to every authority instituted among men: whether to the king, as the supreme authority, or to governors, who are sent by him to punish those who do wrong and to commend those who do right. **1 Peter 2:13–14**

To Husbands

Husbands, in the same way be considerate as you live with your wives, and treat them with respect as the weaker partner and as heirs with you of the gracious gift of life, so that nothing will hinder your prayers. **1 Peter 3:7**

Husbands, love your wives and do not be harsh with them. **Col. 3:19**

To Wives

Wives, submit to your husbands as to the Lord. **Eph. 5:22**

They were submissive to their own husbands, like Sarah, who obeyed Abraham and called him her master. You are her daughters if you do what is right and do not give way to fear. **1 Peter 3:5–6**

To Parents

Fathers, do not exasperate your children; instead, bring them up in the training and instruction of the Lord. **Eph. 6:4**

To Children

Children, obey your parents in the Lord, for this is right. "Honor your father and your mother"—which is the first commandment with a promise—"that it may go well with you and that you may enjoy long life on the earth." **Eph. 6:1–3**

To Workers of All Kinds

Slaves, obey your earthly masters with respect and fear, and with sincerity of heart, just as you would obey Christ. Obey them not only to win their favor when their eye is on you, but like slaves of Christ, doing the will of God from your heart. Serve wholeheartedly, as if you were serving the Lord, not men, because you know that the Lord will reward everyone for whatever good he does, whether he is slave or free. **Eph. 6:5–8**

To Employers and Supervisors

Masters, treat your slaves in the same way. Do not threaten them, since you know that He who is both their Master and yours is in heaven, and there is no favoritism with Him. **Eph. 6:9**

To Youth

Young men, in the same way be submissive to those who are older. All of you, clothe yourselves with humility toward one another, because, "God opposes the proud but gives grace to the humble." Humble yourselves, therefore, under God's mighty hand, that He may lift you up in due time. **1 Peter 5:5–6**

To Widows

The widow who is really in need and left all alone puts her hope in God and continues night and day to pray and to ask God for help. But the widow who lives for pleasure is dead even while she lives. **1 Tim. 5:5–6**

To Everyone

The commandments . . . are summed up in this one rule: "Love your neighbor as yourself." **Rom. 13:9**

I urge . . . that requests, prayers, intercession and thanksgiving be made for everyone. **1 Tim. 2:1**

Let each his lesson learn with care,
and all the household well shall fare.

LUTHER ON HOW TO MEDITATE ON GOD'S WORD

You may certainly use the texts and prayers below at meal times with your family or as brief prayers prayed daily. You may desire, however, to actually use them to learn to meditate on the Word of God. Martin Luther wrote a little book on prayer for his barber, Peter. In it, he lays out his simple method of praying texts. It's brilliant. I call it "I.T.C.P.":

Instruction

Thanksgiving

Confession

Prayer

The method anchors prayer in the texts of Scripture or the catechism but allows the Holy Spirit to prompt thoughts via the Word, which may be chased more freely by the mind at prayer. I recommend this method for the ninety days. It requires a time of solitude, and intentionality. It will also require a period of preparation—perhaps following a brief order for prayer like that found on pages 294–98 of *Lutheran Service Book* (Concordia, 2006) or the inside front cover of *The Lutheran Study Bible* (Concordia, 2009).

Luther gave Peter the barber some examples of how he prayed, but:

> You should also know that I do not want you to re-cite all these words in your prayer. That would make it nothing but idle chatter and prattle, read word for word out of a book as were the rosaries by the laity and the prayers of the priests and monks. Rather do I want your heart to be stirred and guided concerning the thoughts, which ought to be comprehended in the Lord's Prayer. These thoughts may be expressed, if your heart is right-ly warmed and inclined toward prayer, in many differ-ent ways and with more words or fewer. I do not bind myself to such words or syllables, but say my prayers in one fashion today, in another tomorrow, depending upon my mood and feeling. I stay however, as nearly as I can, with the same general thoughts and ideas. It may happen occasionally that I may get lost among so many ideas in one petition that I forego the other six. If such an abundance of good thoughts comes to us we ought to disregard the other petitions, make room for such thoughts, listen in silence, and under no circumstances obstruct them. The Holy Spirit himself preaches here, and one word of his sermon is far better than a thousand of our prayers. Many times I have learned more from one prayer than I might have learned from much read-ing and speculation . . . (AE 43:198).

Luther explains his method, using the Ten Commandments:

> *I think of each commandment as, first, instruction,* which is really what it is intended to be, and consider what the Lord God demands of me so earnestly. Sec-ond, I turn it into a *thanksgiving;* third, a *confession;* and fourth, a *prayer.* I do so in thoughts or words such as these: "I am the Lord your God, etc. You shall have no other gods before me," etc. Here I earnestly consider that God expects and teaches me to trust him sincerely

in all things and that it is his most earnest purpose to be my God. I must think of him in this way at the risk of losing eternal salvation. My heart must not build upon anything else or trust in any other thing, be it wealth, prestige, wisdom, might, piety, or anything else.

Second, I give thanks for his infinite compassion by which he has come to me in such a fatherly way and, un-asked, unbidden, and unmerited, has offered to be my God, to care for me, and to be my comfort, guardian, help, and strength in every time of need. We poor mortals have sought so many gods and would have to seek them still if he did not enable us to hear him openly tell us in our own language that he intends to be our God. How could we ever—in all eternity—thank him enough!

Third, I confess and acknowledge my great sin and ingratitude for having so shamefully despised such sublime teachings and such a precious gift throughout my whole life, and for having fearfully provoked his wrath by countless acts of idolatry. I repent of these and ask for his grace.

Fourth, I pray and say: "O my God and Lord, help me by thy grace to learn and understand thy commandments more fully every day and to live by them in sincere confidence. Preserve my heart so that I shall never again become forgetful and ungrateful, that I may never seek after other gods or other consolation on earth or in any creature, but cling truly and solely to thee, my only God. Amen, dear Lord God and Father. Amen." (AE 43:200)

Works Cited

The Ante-Nicene Fathers. Edited by Alexander Roberts and James Donaldson. 10 vols. 1885–87. Reprinted Grand Rapids: Eerdmans, 1963.

Chemnitz, Martin. *Ministry, Word, and Sacraments: An Enchiridion*. In vol. 5 of Chemnitz's Works. Translated by Luther Poellot. St. Louis: Concordia Publishing House, 2007.

D. Martin Luthers Werke: Kritische Gesamtausgabe. 73 vols. in 85. Weimar: Böhlau, 1883– [Weimarer Ausgabe].

Elert, Werner. *Eucharist and Church Fellowship in the First Four Centuries*. Translated by N. E. Nagel. St. Louis: Concordia Publishing House, 1998.

Kolb, Robert, and Timothy Wengert, eds. *The Book of Concord*. Minneapolis: Fortress Press, 2000.

Lutheran Service Book: Agenda. St. Louis: Concordia Publishing House, 2006.

Peters, Albrecht. *Commentary on Luther's Catechisms: Confession and Christian Life*. Translated by Thomas H. Trapp. St. Louis: Concordia Publishing House, 2013.

———. *Commentary on Luther's Catechisms: Lord's Prayer*. Translated by Daniel Thies. St. Louis: Concordia Publishing House, 2011.

———. *Commentary on Luther's Catechisms: Ten Commandments*. Translated by Holger K. Sonntag. St. Louis: Concordia Publishing House, 2009.

Preus, Robert D. "The Power of God's Word." In *Doctrine Is Life: Essays on Scripture*, edited by Klemet I. Preus, 99–114. St. Louis: Concordia Publishing House, 2006.

A Select Library of Nicene and Post-Nicene Fathers of the Christian Church. Edited by Philip Schaff and Henry Wace. 28 vols. in 2 series. 1886–89. Reprinted Grand Rapids: Eerdmans, 1956.